# INCREDIBLE ART

Sue Nicholson
Deri Robins
Fiona Macdonald

Copyright © QED Publishing, 2008

First published in the UK in 2007 by
QED Publishing
A Quarto Group Company
226 City Road
London EC1V 2TT
www.qed-publishing.co.uk

All rights reserved. No part of this publication may be reproduced, stored in a retrieval system, or transmitted in any form or by any means, electronic, mechanical, photocopying, recording, or otherwise, without the prior permission of the publisher, nor be otherwise circulated in any form of binding or cover other than that in which it is published and without a similar condition being imposed on the subsequent purchaser.

ISBN 978-1-84835-100-4

Written by Sue Nicholson and Deri Robins
Artwork by Melanie Grimshaw and Sarah Morley
Photography by Michael Wicks

Publisher: Steve Evans
Creative Director: Zeta Davies

Printed and bound in China

Web site information is correct at the time of going to press. However, the publishers cannot accept liability for any information or links found on third-party Web sites.

**Picture credits**
Key: t=top, b=bottom, r=right, l=left, c=center
**The Art Archive**/ Eileen Tweedy, Tate Gallery, London 88 tl/ Musée des Art Africains et Océaniens/Dagli Orti/ 143 tr/ 154 tr, 156 t and c, 158 tr and br, 162 cr and br, 172 tr, 174 tr;
**Corbis**/ Rune Hellestad 31 bl/ Douglas Kirkland 42 tl/ Roger De La Harpe, Gallo Images 98 bl/ Caroline Penn 136 tl/ Kevin Fleming 149 tl/ Richard Cummings 152 tr;
**Corbis/Christie's Images**/ Dave G Houser 160 r/ Robert Holmes 165 tc/ 166 tr/ Reza Webistan 170 r/ 176br;
**Getty Images**/ Steve Bly/Stone 145 br/ Bridgeman Art Library 147 cl;
**Japan National Tourist Organisation**/ 168 r;
**Royal Ontario Museum**/ Dinodia 165 tl and c, 166 b;
**Travelsite**/ Neil Setchfield 139 tl, 141 c;
**Werner Forman**/ British Museum 151 tl.

The words in **bold** are explained in the Glossary on page 236.

# Contents

## DRAWING AND CARTOONING

| | |
|---|---|
| Drawing and cartooning kit | 6 |
| Drawing people | 8 |
| Drawing movement | 10 |
| Furry animals | 12 |
| Fish, reptiles and birds | 14 |
| Cities | 16 |
| Countryside | 18 |
| Still life | 20 |
| Self-portrait | 22 |
| Drawing faces | 24 |
| People in poses | 26 |
| Drawing a view | 28 |
| Looking at trees | 30 |
| Cityscapes | 32 |
| Using a grid | 34 |
| Make a dragon head | 36 |
| Cartoon tips and hints | 38 |
| Cartoon figures | 40 |
| Faces and features | 42 |
| On the move | 44 |
| Cartoon creatures | 46 |
| It's alive! | 48 |
| Scary monsters | 50 |
| Set the scene | 52 |
| Comic capers | 54 |
| Make a comic | 56 |

## PAINTING AND PRINTING

| | |
|---|---|
| Painting kit | 58 |
| Printing kit | 60 |
| Splitter splatter! | 62 |
| Straw paintings | 64 |
| Dotty paintings | 66 |
| Wax paintings | 68 |
| Water paintings | 70 |
| From a distance | 72 |
| Paint a Viking stone | 74 |
| Moctezuma's headdress | 76 |
| Abstract art | 78 |
| Painting patterns | 80 |
| Dragging and combing | 82 |
| Watercolour art | 84 |
| Spatter art | 86 |
| Going BIG! | 88 |
| Body prints | 90 |
| Leaf prints | 92 |

# Contents contd...

| | |
|---|---|
| Junk prints | 94 |
| Food prints | 96 |
| Make an Aztec serpent stamp | 98 |
| String prints | 100 |
| Stencil prints | 102 |
| Marbling | 104 |
| Mirror printing | 106 |
| Printing from card | 108 |
| Making blocks | 110 |
| Prints from nature | 112 |
| Potato prints | 114 |
| Make a pop art print | 116 |
| Monoprints | 118 |
| Stencils | 120 |
| Printing pictures | 122 |

## WORLD ART

| | |
|---|---|
| Materials kit | 124 |
| African cloth picture | 126 |
| Egyptian collar | 128 |
| Roman robe clasp | 130 |
| Aboriginal painting | 132 |
| Roman laurel leaf crown | 134 |
| Roman serpent arm bracelet | 136 |
| Chinese paper dragon | 138 |
| Dye material the Viking way | 140 |
| Mexican metapec sun | 142 |
| Ancient world art | 144 |
| Aztec mask | 146 |
| Egyptian amulet | 148 |
| Ancient Greek vase | 150 |
| Roman-style mosaic | 152 |
| Indian Rangoli | 154 |
| Chinese calligraphy | 156 |
| Dress up as an Aztec warrior | 158 |
| Japanese banner | 160 |
| Indonesian puppets | 162 |
| Wear a Jarl's helmet | 164 |
| Stained glass | 166 |
| Moroccan tile | 168 |
| Make your own papyrus paper | 170 |
| Russian egg | 172 |
| Gladiator shield | 174 |

## COLLAGE, SCULPTURE AND SPECIAL EFFECTS

| | |
|---|---|
| Materials kit | 176 |
| 'Me' collage | 178 |
| Magazine collage | 180 |
| Paper collage | 182 |
| Collage face | 184 |
| Food collage | 186 |
| Fabric collage | 188 |
| Nature sculpture | 190 |
| Thumb pot | 192 |
| Aztec monkey pot | 194 |
| Roman plaque | 196 |
| Aztec rain god pendant | 198 |
| Thor's hammer | 200 |
| Clay scultpure | 202 |
| Junk robot | 204 |
| Paper sculpture | 206 |
| Cone hats | 208 |
| Pyramid | 210 |
| Ocean scene | 212 |
| Ocean creatures | 214 |
| Special paint effects | 216 |
| Wax resist | 218 |
| Scraperboard | 220 |
| Wax transfer | 222 |
| Glitter project | 224 |

| | |
|---|---|
| Material world | 226 |
| Paper sewing | 228 |
| Collage | 230 |
| Bits and pieces | 232 |
| Using photos | 234 |
| Glossary | 236 |
| Index | 238 |
| Notes for parents and teachers | 240 |

# Drawing and cartooning kit

coloured pencils

Anyone can create great drawings and cartoons – it's just a matter of learning how to look! But to get started, you'll need some art kit.

Start with a few basic materials: a pad of paper, a couple of pencils and a pencil sharpener. As you learn more, you can try some of the other materials below. Any extra bits and pieces are listed with each project.

## Pencils

You need at least three types of pencil: 2H (a hard pencil, for sharp lines and details); HB (medium hard, for sketching) and 2B (a soft pencil, for drawing guidelines and for **shading**). 4B to 8B pencils are very soft, and are for dark shading.

## Rubber

Not just for deleting: you can use it to make **highlights** in your drawings by revealing the paper underneath.

## Charcoal and chalk

**Charcoal** and **chalk** are great for quick sketches, for large areas of colour and for adding **texture**.

## Oil or chalk pastels

Chalk pastels are soft and crumbly, and give a delicate, blurry effect when you smudge them. Oil pastels make brighter colours.

## Pens and felt-tips

These are perfect for strong black lines or sharp detail. The **nibs** come in many different sizes – you need some thick and some thin ones. Coloured felt-tip pens are good for colouring cartoons.

## Wax crayons

Cheap and good for making bold, colourful pictures and **resist work**.

## Paints and inks

You can use poster paints and inks for making bold, colourful cartoons. **Watercolours** are good for soft colours. Remember, if you use paint or ink, draw your outlines in waterproof pen or they will run when you start painting.

**Paper**

Use scrap paper for your rough ideas and save your best paper for your final drawings. Smooth **sketch paper** is good for pencil and pen drawings. Rough **construction paper** is ideal for pastels, chalk, crayons and charcoal. Experiment with different types, sizes and colours of paper.

**Take care!**
Some projects involve cutting, gluing or spraying. Always ask an adult for help when you see this sign:

# Drawing people

When you draw people, start with simple shapes such as ovals, circles and oblongs.

**1** Draw an oval for the head at the top of your paper.

**2** Add a tube for the neck. Make it almost as wide as the head.

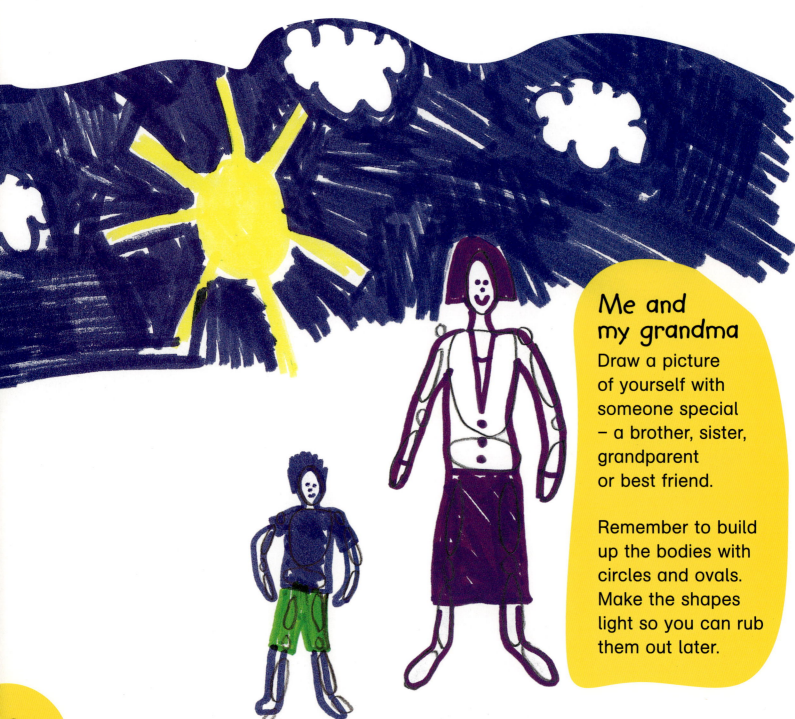

### Me and my grandma

Draw a picture of yourself with someone special – a brother, sister, grandparent or best friend.

Remember to build up the bodies with circles and ovals. Make the shapes light so you can rub them out later.

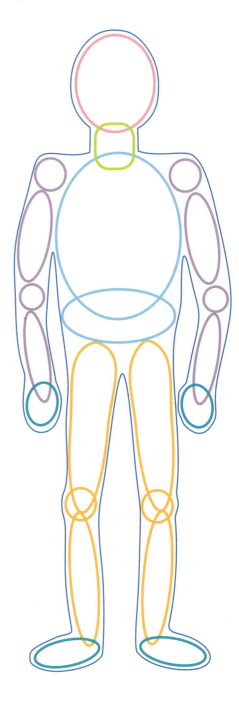

**3** Add a large oval for the top part of the body and a smaller oval for the hips.

**4** Draw circles for the shoulders, oblong shapes for the upper arms, more circles for the elbows, and oblongs for the lower parts of the arms.

**5** Add the legs in the same way. Make the ovals wider at the top. Add circles for knees, then thinner oblong shapes for the shins.

**6** Add simple hand and feet shapes, then finish off with the body's **outline**

**Top tip**
Find photos or cut pictures of people out of magazines. Practise drawing their bodies by using simple shapes.

# Drawing movement

Here's how to make a cardboard figure to help you draw people in different positions.

**Trace these shapes onto tracing paper, then white cardboard**

1 Trace the shapes on the left onto tracing paper, then transfer them to cardboard.

2 Using safety scissors, cut out the cardboard shapes. Push a small hole in each shape with the tip of a ballpoint pen and fasten the shapes together with paper fasteners.

3 Move the parts of your cardboard body so that it looks like it is running, jumping or kicking a ball.

4 Use the figure to help you draw body shapes in different positions, or trace around the figure.

10

## You will need:
- Tracing paper
- White cardboard
- Paper fasteners

# Speed lines

Speed lines will help bring your moving body to life.

**Arrange the figure so the body looks like it is moving naturally**

If you add straight speed lines, the figure will look as if it is flashing past you.

If you add curved speed lines, the figure will look as if it is twirling or twisting around.

**Click for Art!** To see how artists have drawn moving bodies, go to **www.artlex.com** Click on 'Mol–MZ' and scroll down 'movement' or 'motion'.

# Furry animals

You can draw animals in the same way as people, using simple shapes such as circles, ovals and triangles.

**Top tip**
Real animals are hard to draw because they never keep still! Collect animal pictures in a scrapbook so you can look carefully at the animals' shapes.

**1** Draw simple shapes such as circles and ovals first. Make sure the animal's head is smaller than its body.

**2** Draw an outline around the shapes. Rub out lines you no longer need.

**3** Add details such as the ears, eyes, nose and whiskers.

## Drawing fur

To make animals look lifelike, you need to draw the texture of their fur. Here are some different ways.

Velvety-smooth fur drawn with a soft brown oil pastel

Short, spiky fur drawn with a fine felt-tip pen

Soft, fluffy fur drawn with oil pastel

Shaggy fur drawn with scribbled pencils lines

### Click for Art!

For animal drawings by Beatrix Potter, go to www.peterrabbit.co.uk/beatrixpotter/beatrixpotter1c_a.cfm For an outline drawing of a wolf, go to www.tate.org.uk/collection/ and search on 'Henri Gaudier-Brzeska, A Wolf'.

Here are some other furry animals for you to sketch.

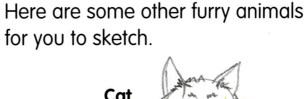

**4** Add colour and texture for the fur. Look at the yellow box for ways of drawing fur.

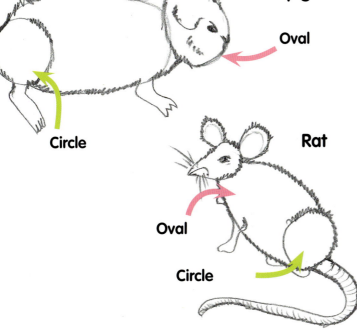

### Top tips

Lines and dots can be smudged with your fingertip to make a cat's fur look soft.

Try rubbing out small areas of shading with a rubber to make highlights.

# Fish, reptiles and birds

You can draw fish, reptiles and birds in the same way as cats and dogs, using simple shapes.

## Top tip
Birds are the easiest pets to draw – all you need is a circle for the head, an oval body, and a long pointed tail.

## Bird
1. Draw a circle and an oval.
2. Add the wing and tail shapes.
3. Add the eye, beak and feet.

## Fish face
1. Draw an oval head.
2. Draw two bulging eyes on both sides, and a curved mouth.
3. Add the tail and fins.

## Snake
1. Start with a simple curved line.
2. Draw the rest of the body.
3. Add the snake's eye, tongue and markings.

# Scales and feathers

Scales can be drawn neatly, in rows. Notice how scales often overlap each other. You can add some shading, too.

Use long, straight lines to draw large feathers on a bird's wings and tail.

Use short, curved lines to draw short, soft feathers on a bird's head and chest.

## Lizard
1. Draw two ovals and a tail.
2. Add the legs.
3. Draw patterns on the lizard's body. Don't forget its tongue!

## Turtle
1. Draw half an oval for the shell and the head.
2. Add the legs and neck.
3. Draw markings on the shell and legs.

**Click for Art!** To see children's drawings of birds and snakes, go to **www.junglephotos.com/** Search under 'children's artwork' then follow the link.

# Cities

City streets are full of exciting shapes. Follow the steps below to make your own city scene.

**You will need:**
- A large sheet of sketch paper
- Wax crayons or pastels
- A soft pencil
- A ruler

### Top tip
The next time you visit a big city, look carefully at the buildings. What do you notice about the shapes of doors, windows and roofs?

**1** Lightly sketch the outline of different buildings across the bottom of the paper.

**2** Draw taller buildings behind. Use a ruler to keep your lines straight.

# City at night

This picture of a city at night has been drawn with bright red, yellow, white and blue crayons on black paper.

Curved sides of buildings make the picture look more exciting

Tiny coloured dashes for lit-up windows

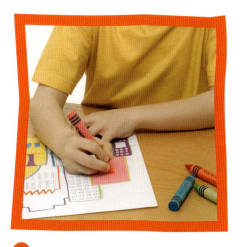

**3** Sketch in building details, such as doors and windows. Make details smaller in the **background**, so some buildings look farther away.

**4** Go over the outlines of your buildings in wax crayons or pastels. Use a different colour for each building.

**5** Colour in the rest of your picture using strong, bright colours. Paint a blue sky behind your city, or cut out a row of buildings and glue it to a sheet of coloured paper.

**Click for Art!** To see Robert Delaunay's 'The Red Tower', go to www.artchive.com/artchive/D/delaunay/red_tower.jpg.html

17

# Countryside

In the country, shapes are rounded and softer than in the city. Follow the steps to draw a scene with different tree shapes and rounded hills.

You will need:
- A large sheet of sketch paper
- Coloured chalks, pastels or crayons

1 Lightly sketch the shape of the trees (look at the green box for help).

**2** Draw the rounded hills. Make them smaller as they get farther away.

**3** Draw the shapes of smaller trees in the distance.

**4** Colour in the drawing with chalks, pastels or crayons.

# Drawing trees

**1** Lightly sketch the trunk and outline of the tree.

**2** Draw the main branches. Make each branch thick near the trunk and thinner at the ends.

**3** Use different shades of green for the leaves. Make the top leaves pale and the lower leaves dark, where it is more shady.

**Click for Art!**

To see a landscape by Monet, go to **www.ibiblio.org/wm/paint/auth/monet/** and click on 'First Impressionist paintings'.

# Still life

A still life is a drawing or painting of something that does not move, such as flowers in a vase or a bowl of fruit.

**1** Take time arranging the fruit in a bowl or on a tabletop until you are happy with the way it looks.

**2** Lightly sketch the outline of the bowl first, then draw the fruit. Start with the pieces at the front of the bowl.

### You will need:
- Something to draw, such as a bowl of fruit or a flower
- Coloured pencils, chalks, crayons or pastels

**Tiny lines give the orange peel a rough texture**

**Shading makes the fruit look rounded and three-dimensional**

**3** Draw the pieces of fruit at the back. Only draw the parts of the fruit you can see.

**4** Go over your outlines in crayon, chalk or pastel.

**5** Colour in or shade your picture.

### Top tip

Before you start, look carefully at what you are going to draw. It sounds obvious, but many people who try to draw don't do that!

**A colourful still life of flowers in a vase**

### Click for Art!

To see still-life paintings by Cézanne, go to
www.ibiblio.org/wm/paint/auth/cezanne/sl/

# Self-portrait

One of the best ways to learn how to sketch people's faces is to draw pictures of yourself. First sketch a quick self-portrait from memory on scrap paper.

**Perfect portraits**

Is your face round, oval, heart-shaped, square or long? If you can't tell, use a soft pencil or crayon and trace the shape of your face on a mirror – then you can look at the outline and tell what shape it is.

Before you start your self-portrait, think about your features. What shape are your eyes? Are your lips thin or full? Is your nose long or short?

Follow the steps on page 23. Look carefully at your reflection and draw a picture of your face. Think about the **shading** and **texture**.

Compare it with the first sketch you did – you'll be amazed how much better your new drawing is!

Start by looking carefully at yourself in the mirror. Think about where your ears are in relation to your eyes and nose.

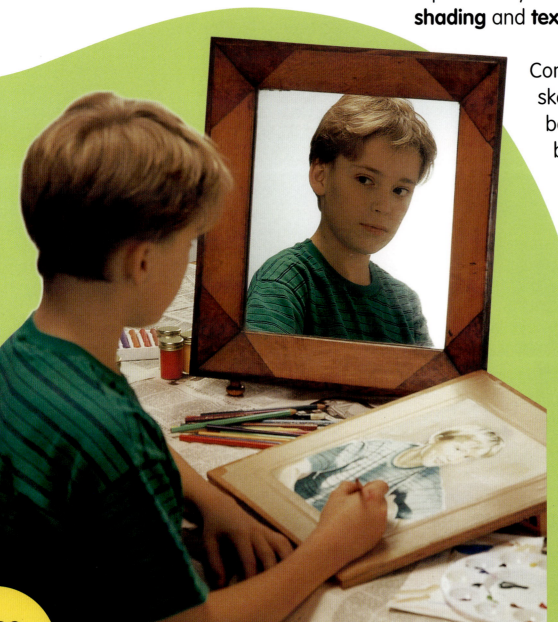

Follow these steps to help you get all your features in the right place:

**1** Use a soft pencil to sketch a faint egg shape for the **outline** of your face.

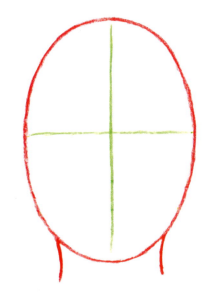

**2** Draw a line down the middle of the face, and another one just above the centre from side to side.

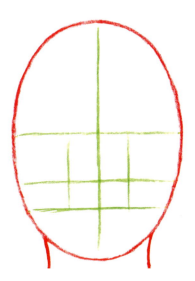

**3** Now divide the lower half into two. Then draw three more lines: one across and two up and down as shown.

**4** Use the lines as a guide to sketch in your eyes. Leave one eye width between them. Draw your mouth: start with the line between the lips, then add the outline of the upper and lower lips. Draw in the tip of your nose, but not the sides.

**5** Add your ears, hair, eyelashes, eyebrows, chin and other details. Now you can add shading and colour with coloured pencils.

23

# Drawing faces

When you feel confident about drawing yourself, try drawing other people. Faces come in all shapes and sizes, and everyone's features are different. You can build up hundreds of different faces by making an Identikit set.

## Identikit set

**1** Draw four or five different face shapes, and divide them into sections.

**2** Now cut lots of strips of paper, each the same width as the sections in the face.

**3** Draw different-shaped eyes on some of the strips, noses on others and mouths on the rest, all with different expressions.

**4** Now mix and match the features on the different faces. You can cut out hairlines, moustaches and glasses, too.

**5** When you've created a face you like, trace or copy the outline and features onto another piece of paper. Use coloured pencils to turn it into a finished drawing.

### Art file
People don't smile all the time! Collect photos and newspaper cuttings of faces with different expressions, and practise drawing them.

## Egg heads

It's not quite as easy to draw people's faces from the side, or from above or below! A hard-boiled egg can be a very useful part of your art kit.

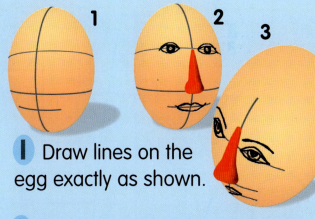

**1** Draw lines on the egg exactly as shown.

**2** Draw in the features. Stick a blob of clay on for the nose.

**3** Using your egg-head as a model, practise drawing faces from different angles.

# People in poses

When you're drawing a figure, think of the head as an egg, and the arms and legs as sausages or tubes. Use this technique to draw people in different poses.

**1** Start with the head at the top of your paper. Draw an egg shape.

**2** Add a short tube for the neck. It should be almost as wide as the head.

**3** Now draw an egg shape for the top of the body.

**4** Draw the arms as if they were two sausage shapes joined in the middle.

**5** Draw the rest of the body using egg shapes and circles.

**6** Draw the legs in the same way as the arms, but make them wider at the top.

**7** Finally, add simple hand and feet shapes and draw the final outline to your figure.

Now draw your sausage and egg figures sitting, lying or crawling. Look at people in different poses or from different angles to get some ideas.

### Try this

If you draw these shapes roughly first of all, you can add the details later. Sketch lightly with a soft pencil. Rub out the original lines when your drawing is complete.

# Make a poster

Find some photos of your favourite sports, film or pop star, and draw him or her by building up from simple shapes.

Use different pens, pencils and crayons for your picture. What different effects can you create? Remember to use shading for the dark areas and leave **highlights** for the light areas.

# Drawing a view

When it comes to drawing a view, how do you decide which bits to put in, and which to leave out? Making a viewfinder can help you to decide.

**Make a viewfinder**

A viewfinder is a piece of cardboard with a hole in the middle. Make it out of two L-shaped pieces of cardboard, and you can change the shape to make a square or a rectangle.

1 Cut an L-shape out of cardboard. Trace around it to make an identical shape, and cut this one out, too.

2 Use paperclips to hold the pieces together and make a rectangle.

1

2

### Top tip

Silver or white pencils look good on black **construction paper**. Use black pens or felt-tips to draw **silhouettes** – such as a winter **landscape** or a sunset. Silhouettes are solid dark **outlines** on a lighter **background**. They look good against soft white tissue paper or silver backgrounds.

1

## Using the viewfinder

**1** Hold the viewfinder in front of you. Look through the hole in the middle as if it were a camera lens. Move it around until you find the right view. What happens when you look at the same view **horizontally** and **vertically**?

**2** When you have chosen your view, quickly sketch the main parts of the picture with a soft pencil (you can rub it out afterwards) using one hand. This is your rough outline for the finished picture to indicate large areas, such as grass, sky or water. Sketch in the position of any buildings or trees.

**3** When you have done the outlines, put the viewfinder away and finish the picture, putting in the details and using coloured pencils, chalks or pastels.

2

3

29

# Looking at trees

As with all your drawings, it is important to look carefully at a tree before you try to draw it. Notice how the branches grow from one another, rather than all coming straight from the trunk.

**Some trees have long branches that reach out the side**

There are a huge variety of tree shapes.

**Some trees are very tall and thin.**

### Up Close
Bark varies a lot, too. Rubbings are a great way to collect different types of bark for reference. Put a piece of white paper over a section of the trunk and rub the surface with a soft pencil or crayon.

It can help to sketch the overall shape of a tree before you draw in the detail. Try filling the whole piece of paper with your tree shape to make it really dramatic.

**1** Lightly sketch in the trunk and the overall outline of the tree.

**2** Draw the main branches, making them thinner at the ends.

**3** Add fine lines for the smaller twigs, right up to the edge of the outline.

This is how the tree looks in winter, but deciduous trees change throughout the whole year. Leaves appear, change colour and fall; buds can be followed by blossoms and then berries.

Soft pencils or charcoal are ideal for drawing wintry trees. For a dramatic effect, use white chalk on black paper. Just colour the spaces around the tree, and in between the branches, to make dramatic **silhouettes**.

# Cityscapes

A cityscape is a view of a city. Don't worry that buildings are too complicated to draw – the trick is to look at everything carefully and to build up the picture from patterns and shapes.

**1** Decide what you are going to put into your picture. Are there any interesting buildings in your area? Use your viewfinder to help you decide which is the best view. You could use a scene from a postcard or from a book.

**2** First, draw the outlines on a wide piece of paper. Look carefully at the buildings – are they wider than they are tall? Do the roofs slope steeply or are they shallow?

**3** When you have done the outlines, sketch in the doors and windows. Check how big they are compared with the rest of the building.

**4** Add the other details, such as chimneys, turrets, porches, steps, stones, wood and brick patterns. Finish by adding colour, using white to create highlights for bright spots.

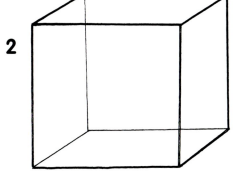

# Build your own

To make a building look three-dimensional, you need to draw its side view in addition to its front.

**1** Draw the front of the building.

**2** Draw in the sides, to make a **cube**.

**3** Add a roof, door and windows.

**4** Shade the side of the house lightly – you could add a shadow to make it look realistic.

# Using a grid

Drawing is about looking and copying exactly what you see. Sometimes our mind tricks us and we draw what we expect to see, not what is actually in front of us. Using a grid can help you get the **proportions** exactly right and can also help you make your pictures larger or smaller.

1 Take a photo or magazine cutting, and trace the outline of the picture you want to copy onto tracing paper. Now divide your tracing into equal squares, using a ruler to help you.

2 Take a sheet of paper, and make the same number of squares using a soft pencil. You can make the squares the same size as the ones on the tracing paper, or they can be smaller or bigger.

3 Copy the main outlines of the picture into each square one by one. Concentrate on each square at a time, rather than looking at the whole picture.

**Upside-down drawing**

Choose a picture from a magazine that you'd like to draw, and draw a grid over it. Make a separate grid on a sheet of white paper. Turn the original picture upside down. Now copy each square, including all the **shading**. Your finished picture will be much more accurate, because you are just copying areas of colour and shade, rather than trying to draw the details.

**Using a piece of wallpaper lining, make a big poster of an animal for your wall. Use the grid technique with chalks or charcoals to fill in large areas quickly.**

**4** When the main outline is complete, rub out the guidelines and fill in the smaller details, using the photo as a guide.

# Make a Dragon Head

Dragons appear in a lot of Viking art because they are fierce, wild and mysterious – just like famous Viking heroes.

### You will need:
- Tracing paper
- Pencil
- Ruler
- Cardstock
- Black and white paint
- Paintbrushes
- Craft knife

This 70 ½ foot (21.5 metre) long wooden ship has a snake-shaped prow. It was made in Norway more than 1,000 years ago.

A snarling magic beast, carved in wood. It was found in the ship above. Similar carvings were used on the prows of Viking warships.

**1** Draw a grid of 1 inch (2 centimetre) squares onto tracing paper. Put the grid over the dragon, left, and draw around it.

36

**2** On a cardstock sheet, draw a large grid of 4 x 4 inch (10 x 10 centimetre) squares. Both grids need the same number of squares.

**3** Copy the contents of each square on the tracing paper grid into the matching square on the big grid.

**4** Mix white and black paint to make grey. Paint your dragon head and leave it to dry completely.

**5** Ask an adult to cut out your dragon head. Draw on the dragon's features. Go over with black paint.

### Did you know?
In winter, when rivers, lakes and bogs were frozen, Vikings travelled on sleds, skates and skis.

# Cartoon tips and hints

Anyone can draw cartoons – the more you practise, the better you'll become! Start with a person, an animal or an object, or use your imagination to create a fantasy character or monster.

### What is a cartoon?
What makes cartoons different from other drawings? Think about your favourite cartoon character from films, television, comic strips or picture books.

*The Simpsons*, **created by Matt Groening, is known the world over.**

## Animal magic
Look carefully at different animals and make sketches of them. Look at books, magazines or websites on the Internet. You could also watch wildlife programmes on television, or use a microscope to look at tiny insects.

## People pictures

Look carefully at your family, friends or favourite celebrity. Everyone has a unique **feature** that would make a great cartoon. Collect photos of people in different outfits, positions and poses. Look at them for ideas when you draw your cartoons.

## Cool cartoons

You can get different effects depending on which tools you use. Use a black pen or felt-tip to outline and shade your cartoons. Felt-tips create bold outlines and flat colour. Coloured inks give a softer effect. Combine a black ink outline with pencils, coloured ink or **watercolours**.

# Cartoon figures

The easiest way to draw a cartoon figure is to sketch a simple outline first, and then add the details. You can start by drawing stick figures or round people. Begin by trying the cartoon figure below.

**Stick figures**

**1** Draw a stick figure with oval head, hands and feet. Put small circles at the joints.

**2** Build up the figure by adding more ovals for the body, such as for the shoulders and hips.

**3** Draw in the basic features of the face.

**4** Finish by adding details for the face and clothing. Last of all, fill in with colour.

### Top tip
You can use circles and ovals to make cartoon figures: stretched ovals make tall, skinny cartoons, circles make plump people. Mix the two to create fat people with spindly legs.

# Big and little

To draw a cartoon of somebody you know, look at them carefully. Are they tall or short? Fat or thin? Now exaggerate their most outstanding feature. Practise drawing from photographs.

**1** Draw the outline of your figure using circles or ovals.

**2** Now add details to make them funny, such as hair, shoes and clothes.

# Faces and features

Faces and **expressions** are important in cartoons. Start at the top. First draw the head shapes, then add the different features. You can easily make your cartoon character look ahead or sideways.

**Head On**

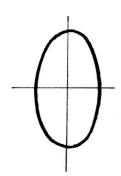

1 Draw an oval. Divide it into quarters.

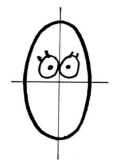

2 Put in the eyes just above the centre.

3 Add the nose on the centre line. Add the mouth halfway down.

4 Add hair, eyebrows and eyelashes. Make your faces happy, sad or scared.

### Top tip
Try different face shapes: long and thin, short and fat! Fat heads have no neck. Thin heads look skinnier on a long, thin neck.

Hair can make a big difference to your characters. Different styles can make characters look messy or glamorous, young or old.

If you are making someone you know into a cartoon, look at them carefully. What do you notice most about them? Do they have a long chin? A wide face? Ears that stick out? A big nose? Glasses? These are the features you can exaggerate to make a great cartoon.

Remember glasses and jewellery. Details bring cartoons to life.

### Top tip

Look at your reflection in the back of a serving spoon. With your face in the light against a dark background, draw what you see. Your face will be stretched and distorted. Copy this for an instant cartoon effect.

43

# On the move

Now you've created your cartoon characters, you need to make them move. Follow the hints and tips below to get them running, jumping and even flying.

**Head On!**

1. Begin with a simple figure.

2. Then add ovals and circles.

3. Now add clothes, colour and facial **expressions**.

**Jumping**

Running

Movement lines help to show which way something is moving – and how fast.

**Top tip**
Movement lines also add extra action to your cartoon – just look at the pictures below. Adding double movement lines behind these figures makes them look more active.

# Cartoon creatures

Before you start drawing cartoon animals, practise sketching real ones. Then try turning your sketches into cartoons.

**Drawing animals**

Notice the features and **personalities** of a variety of animals. A dog's ears can be droopy or perky, depending on whether it is happy or sad.

**Kooky Animals**

You can build up any kind of animal from simple shapes:

# Animal shapes

1. Draw an outline of the head and body, using circles and ovals. Add the legs, feet and tail.

2. Rub out the guide lines that you don't want in the final picture.

3. Use coloured pencils or pens to finish the drawing.

When you are confident about drawing animals, try stretching the body and limbs to make them taller and skinnier, or squash them for rounder, fatter, more comical, cartoon creatures.

**Create a new animal star**
Some animals have been turned into cartoons many times before – especially bears and cats! Try to think of something more unusual and see what you can do with it. Will it be fierce or friendly? Smart or stupid? Fast or slow?

# It's alive!

Cartoons can make anything come to life. Look around your bedroom for inspiration – or your garden or classroom. You can make your whole street into cartoon characters.
The windows can be the eyes of the houses and the doors can be mouths.

**Kitchen cartoons**

Choose an object and get to know it well. Draw it so often, and from so many different angles, that it becomes as familiar as a friend.

Give it a name and turn its parts into human features: a spout or handle can become a nose, for example.

48

**Motor mouths**

Give bikes, cars, scooters, skateboards, boats, trains and buses funny faces to bring them to life. Try to make the shapes match the expressions – for example, a car can be round, smiley and friendly, or long, low and aggressive, with a long radiator that looks like a mouthful of flashing teeth, and evil eyes instead of headlights.

49

# Scary monsters

People, animals, buildings or houses can make scary cartoons – and that's even before you start drawing the real monsters, such as vampires, werewolves and ghosts!

Everyone will recognize a vampire. How about making up your own monsters?

Wicked witches are usually ugly and have pointed noses, long chins and warts on their faces.

1   2   3

You can make ghosts as black silhouettes, or as white, cloudy shapes with a soft, black outline in the shape of a whirlwind.

### Monster tip
Try mixing parts of different animals into a new fantasy friend or **fiend.**

**A question of size**
Even tiny creatures can become terrifying if they grow to a huge size.

**Mythical monsters**
**Myths** and **legends** are full of strange and scary creatures, such as dragons, werewolves and devils. Choose a mythical monster and turn it into a cartoon. Will yours be scary, friendly or funny?

51

# Set the scene

After you've created a group of cartoon characters, it's fun to put them in different backgrounds. Use real-life situations or invent a fantasy world – your background can be more interesting than a blank piece of paper.

### Top tip
Always start by sketching your cartoon character in soft pencil first, and then add the background. Add **foreground** details last. When you are happy with the finished result, colour it in and go over the **outlines** in thick, black pen.

### Where to get ideas
Look at travel magazines, photos and books, or around your house, street or school – which of these scenes suit your cartoon characters? Draw some simple backgrounds – choose a few details that show where the location is meant to be.

**Placing your character**
Your character should appear to be part of the scene, not just stuck on top of it – make sure that there is some detail in front of it as well as behind it.

**Night or day?**
Nighttime backgrounds are great for a spooky atmosphere. Draw your character and buildings in black silhouette.

**In the mood**
Different skies set the mood, too. It's easy to fill the sky with snow or rain!

# Comic capers

Now that you've learned how to draw amazing cartoon figures, you can put them in your own comic story. First, take a look at some of your favourite comics. You'll see that the pages are split into **frames** of different sizes and shapes.

Frames don't have to be square! Try circles, ovals and ones with jagged edges. You can draw the frames by hand so that they are not all straight lines or draw them neatly with a ruler. Comic strips look more exciting if parts of the picture break out of the frame edges.

**Storylines**

Your characters can 'talk' in speech and thought bubbles. If you need extra information, and have enough space, you can put words in boxes at the top or bottom of the picture. Speech bubbles are usually oval. Bubbles that look like clouds are used to show a character's thoughts. Jagged bubbles are for angry people, and shivery bubbles can be used for a character who is scared.

**Exclamation marks!**

These punctuation marks are used a lot in comics! To show people shouting, use a thick black marker.

**Bubbles tip**

Speech and thought bubbles usually go in the top third of the picture, so draw your sketch in the bottom two-thirds.

# Make a comic

Now that you've seen how it's done, try creating a comic strip with your own cast of funny, scary or silly characters. You can even make a whole comic book from a collection of strips.

YOUR CARTOON CHARACTER CAN DO ANYTHING!

### Lights, camera, action!

Making a comic strip is like making a film: you need a story, a main character, a few minor characters and a series of backgrounds. Start by thinking up a short, simple story with a beginning, a middle and an end. Look through some joke books for a funny ending.

### Stars of the show

What will your main character look like? Decide what sort of personality they have and think of a name. Try drawing them from lots of different angles to get them right. You also need friends and enemies for the main character to talk to. Try not to have more than three characters, otherwise readers may get confused.

## Storyboarding

You're ready to make a storyboard. This is a rough sketch of each frame; it doesn't have to be perfect. Try to vary the pictures. Sometimes characters can be in the distance, other times you can show a close-up of their face and expression.

## Comic frames

When you are happy with your storyboard, turn it into a finished comic strip. Draw each box neatly, with a ruler and pencil. Make sure you draw the frames big enough to fit in all the details you want.

## Finishing off

Copy your drawings from the storyboard and turn them into finished cartoons. First, draw the outlines in pencil.

Go over the outlines with black marker or felt-tip. Colour in the pictures with paint or felt-tips. Your comic is complete!

57

**Coloured pencils**

# Painting kit

You only need brushes and a paint set to create great pictures but with a few extra materials you will also be able to experiment with exciting effects.

**Top tip**
Collect old jam jars to hold water to wash your brushes in.

**Pencils**

**Pencils**

Soft-lead pencils (such as 9B) are useful for sketching the outlines of your pictures before adding paint. Use coloured pencils to add detail.

**Basic equipment**
- Paper and poster paper
- Poster, **acrylic** paper **watercolour paints**
- Pencils and paintbrushes
- Safety scissors
- White glue

You will also need some extra items, which are listed separately for each project.

**Brushes**

Different brushes give different results. You need a fine, pointed one for details, a middle thickness one and a really thick one for large areas. Nylon bristles are best for thin paint, and hogs' hair brushes are better for thick paint. Use an old toothbrush for spattering, and sponges and rags for dabbing.

**Palettes and pots**

You can buy artists' **palettes** for mixing colours – but an old plastic tray, an old plate or piece of smooth wood are just as good. Use jars full of water to clean your brushes.

Brushes

Palette

Watercolours

Acrylic paints

Ink

Gouache paints

## Paint

Poster paints are ideal for big, bold paintings, or to mix with other things to create texture. Use them straight from the container or thin them down with water. Watercolours are delicate colours that make great landscapes. They come in tubes or blocks, are easy to carry and handy for colour sketches. Gouache paints produce strong, vibrant colours that are good to use on coloured papers.

## Paper

It's important to use good paper. Smooth **sketch paper** is best. The paint doesn't sink into the surface and rough construction paper can be interesting. watercolour paper is thick, so that it doesn't wrinkle when it gets wet.

Art paper

Poster paints

# Printing kit

This section will show you how to make fantastic prints from cardboard, sponges, leaves – even food. You can find almost everything you need from around the house.

## Basic equipment
- Paper and cardboard
- Poster/**acrylic** paints
- Pencils and paintbrushes
- Safety scissors
- White glue
- Ruler

You will also need the extra items listed separately for each project.

**Paper and cardboard**

You can make prints on white or coloured paper, cardstock, posterboard or cardboard.

**Printing blocks**

You can make printing blocks from craft foam, sponges or cardboard.

**Paints for printing**

The best paints to use are poster paints or acrylic paints. Use fabric paints for printing on cloth.

Don't forget to spread some newspaper to work on, and to wear an apron to keep your clothes clean.

### Take care!
Some projects involve cutting, ironing and photocopying. Always ask an adult for help where you see this sign:

### Craft supplies
Keep a big box full of things you can use to make prints. Look out for items with interesting textures or shapes. For example:
- ★ the end of heavyweight corrugated cardboard
- ★ an old sponge or cork
- ★ a piece of yarn
- ★ bubble wrap
- ★ a Lego® brick
- ★ a feather

**Brushes and paint dishes**

You will need different-sized paintbrushes and old dishes for mixing your paints.

A printing roller is also useful for spreading paint evenly on a flat surface.

# Splitter splatter!

Make a lively painting by spattering paint onto paper with a brush or toothbrush.

**You will need:**
An old toothbrush

**1** Draw fish and starfish outlines on a sheet of paper. Turn the paper over and place it face down on some newspaper.

**2** Dip a toothbrush in yellow paint, then drag your finger over the bristles to spatter the paint on the paper. Try flicking yellow and orange paint with ordinary brushes, too.

**3** Now flick blue and green paint onto a second sheet of paper. Use different shades of blue and green to make a speckled sea background.

**Top tip**
Paint spattering is messy! Wear an apron, and spread out plenty of newspaper to work on.

**Follow the steps above to create this speckly underwater scene.**

**Click for Art!** To see 'drip paintings' by the American artist Jackson Pollock, go to http://www.artlex.com/ and search for 'Action painting'.

**4** When the paint is dry, turn the paper over and cut out the fish and starfish with safety scissors. Arrange them on your sea background and glue them down.

# Desert landscape

**1** Make cardboard **stencils** using the shapes below.

**2** Arrange the stencils on a sheet of thick white paper. Use a small dab of glue to hold them in place.

**3** Spatter yellow paint over the bottom part of the paper for the sand. Spatter blue paint above for the sky.

**4** When the paint is dry, remove the cardboard stencils.

**Copy these shapes onto poster paper to create the desert landscape above.**

# Straw paintings

Blowing paint through a straw makes the paint wander in wiggly lines and creates wonderful and unusual shapes.

**Top tip**
To mix colours, add a second colour when the first is still wet. If you do not want your colours to mix, wait until the first colour is dry before you add another.

**You will need:**
A plastic drinking straw

**1** Add water to some poster or acrylic paint to make the paint runny.

**2** Drip a large blob of paint onto your paper with a brush.

**3** Gently blow the paint through the straw. The paint will spread across the paper in wiggly lines.

**4** Add different colours one by one. (See Top tip for hints on colour mixing.)

Sometimes a straw painting may start to look like something recognizable – such as a fluffy chick, a flower, a person's hair or an insect.

**This straw painting was made into a tree by adding a trunk with a brush.**

**This chick's legs, eyes and beak were added with pencil and orange crayon.**

**5** Add details with a crayon or brush to complete your painting.

### Click for Art!

To explore paintings by Jackson Pollock, Mark Rothko and Robert Rauschenberg, go to **www.sfmoma.org/anderson/** Click on 'Start Project' and then 'Explore 15 works'.

# Dotty paintings

To blend colours, try using a pattern of different-coloured dots and dashes.

**You will need:** A paintbrush with a fine tip

## Mixing colours

**1** Before you begin your picture, practise making lots of tiny dots next to each other with the tip of your brush. Try one colour first, such as red.

**2** Now make some more red dots on a clean sheet of paper. This time, space the dots out a little.

**3** When the red paint is dry, add yellow dots in between. Stand back. What colour do the red and yellow dots look like from a distance?

Pink and turquoise dashes

**4** Now try making dots and dashes with different colours and different-sized brushes.

Dark purple and lilac dots

Blue and red blobs

# Frog on a lily pad

Yellow dots highlight the frog's back

**Top tip**
Make darker dots and place them closer together to add detail and shading.

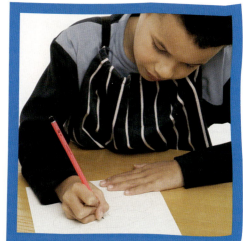

**1** Plan your painting in your sketchbook or on a piece of scratch paper.

**2** Lightly sketch the outline of your painting on a sheet of white paper.

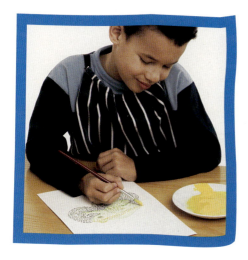

**3** Colour each part of the picture with tiny dots of colour. This dotty painting has dark green for the lily pads, pale green for the frog and yellow and dark green dots for the frog's markings.

**Click for Art!**
To learn how the French painter Seurat made paintings out of tiny dots, go to www.metmuseum.org/Works_of_Art/ and search for 'Circus Sideshow'.

67

# Wax paintings

Use paint and wax crayons to make wax **resist** paintings. The wax resists the paint, so the colour of the crayons shows through.

**1** Cover the bottom of your paper with a white crayon for snow.

**You will need:**
- Thick paper or poster paper
- Wax crayons
- Blue watercolour or poster paint

**2** Still using crayons, add a snowman in the middle. Give him an orange carrot nose, two eyes, a black hat, some buttons and a striped scarf.

**3** Add white crayon dots for falling snow.

**4** Mix dark blue paint for the background. If you are using poster paint, add water to make it thinner.

# Scraper effects

**1** With wax crayons, create patches of bright colour on thick paper.

**2** Paint three layers of black, dark blue or purple acrylic paint over the crayon patches.

### Top tip
If you are making a scraper picture, be sure to use thick paper or cardboard, as ordinary paper may tear.

**3** When the paint is dry, scrape a picture into the paint with a knitting needle. The bright colours will show through.

**5** Brush the blue paint over your drawing. The crayon marks will resist the paint, so your drawing stands out.

# Lost in space!

To make this picture, draw the rocket, planets and stars first using bright crayons. Then add black watercolour paint on top.

# Water paintings

Enjoy experimenting with watercolour paints. They are great for seas and skies!

**You will need:**
- Watercolour paper
- Watercolour paints
- A wide brush
- A thin, pointed brush
- A sponge, tissue paper or cotton balls

1. With a brush, paint clean water all over your sheet of watercolour paper.

2. Paint yellow stripes over the top half of your paper. Add orange stripes halfway down.

3. Paint the sea using shorter brushstrokes. Use orange, yellow and blue. Let the colours run a little.

**Top tip**
To help the colours in the sea run together, drip a few drops of clean water over the paint.

**4** While the paint is still wet, dab a cotton ball on the yellow sky so the patches look like pale clouds.

**5** When the paint is dry, paint a black island and a palm tree. If you want, add a shark's fin pointing out of the water!

# Watery skies

For cloudy skies, paint overlapping stripes of blue watercolour paint across your paper. Before the paint dries, dab it with a clean sponge. This will leave white patches that look like clouds.

**These clouds were made by painting stripes of blue across wet paper, then dabbing the paint with scrunched-up tissue paper.**

For a different effect, let the blue paint dry, then paint clouds in white watercolour paint.

**Click for Art!**

To see watercolours by the English artist Turner, go to www.j-m-w-turner.co.uk/ Click on 'Turner in Venice', scroll down, then click on the small pictures.

71

# From a distance

Ever since the first artist picked up a brush, people have tried to paint the world around them. This project will help you capture lots of different views in your paintings.

**Paint a 3-D theatre**

This **3-D** theatre is made up of cards, one behind the other, to make the scenery look convincing. Just as in a painting, you should make the front scenery strong using bold colours and the faraway parts paler.

You will need:
- Thin cardboard
- A ruler and pencils
- Scissors
- Crayons and paint

**1** Cut two squares of cardboard, each 7 inches (17 ½ centimetres) square. Use a ruler to divide them into ten ¾-inch (2 centimetre) lines.

**3** Glue the accordian sides onto a cardboard base. Cut out five rectangles, each 7 x 9 inches (17 ½ x 22 ½ centimetres). Paint one blue for the sky. Glue it to the sides to make the **backdrop**. Cut another rectangle into a frame shape and glue it to the front.

**2** Fold along the lines to make two **accordian** shapes for the sides of your theatre.

**4** The three remaining rectangles are for your scenery. Draw a country scene on one softly in pencil, with a house at the top. The other two pieces should be rolling hedges. Draw these so that they are not as tall as the house scenery. The smaller scenes will slot in the front.

**5** Now colour the scenery. Remember to use soft, pale colours in the distance, and strong, sharp details at the front. Finally, cut the pieces out, ready to slot into place in your 3-D theatre.

**Create different sets of scenery for your theatre. What about a city at night?**

**6** Slot the cards into the theatre in the right order. This will show you how you can create a sense of distance in your paintings.

# Paint a Viking Stone

The Vikings painted stones to record their history and stories of gods and monsters. Make your own Viking stone in five easy steps.

## You will need:
- Smooth stone or pebble
- Chalk or white pencil
- Acrylic paints
- Paint brushes
- Gold metallic pen
- Acrylic varnish or pva mixture (3 parts pva, 1 part water)

### Did you know?
These are all Viking words: both, drag, egg, fall, gale, knife, score, scold, ship, sling, slug, smile, want, whirl, whistle, window and wing.

The Viking homelands in northern Europe were surrounded by stormy seas to the east, west and south, and by Arctic ice to the north.

Monster face with horns and a long beard carved on a stone in Viking Denmark.

**1** Find a smooth stone or pebble in the yard or park. Wash it in soapy water, rinse and leave to dry.

**2** With a white pencil or chalk, carefully copy the picture on the opposite page onto your stone.

**3** Paint the face blue, except for the eyes and mouth. Paint the mouth red and add a white dot on each side.

**4** Paint the eyes light blue. Once all the paint is dry, use a gold metallic pen to go over your lines.

**5** Use a clean brush to add a coat of PVA mixture as varnish. Leave to dry, then add another coat.

**Use your stone as a paperweight or display it on a shelf.**

75

# Moctezuma's headdress

Aztec rulers wore splendid headdresses made of priceless feathers and gold. Now you can wear one, too!

Making a feather fan (left) and a feather headdress (right).

This headdress probably belonged to the great Aztec ruler, Moctezuma (Mock-th-zoh-mah).

### You will need:
- Compass
- Cardstock
- Pencil
- Ruler
- Scissors
- Paint and paintbrushes
- Gold glitter glue
- Green, blue and turquoise paper
- Tape

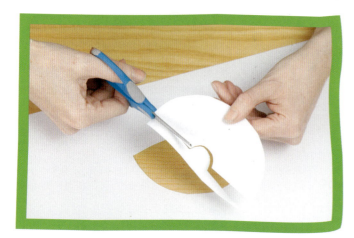

**1** Set your compass to 3 inches (7.5 centimetres) Draw a semicircle and cut out. Cut out a smaller one in the center.

**2** Paint on stripes of blue, green and brown for feathers. When dry, add dots of gold using glitter glue.

**3** Make a feather template. Use it to draw and cut out 12 feathers from some blue and green paper.

**4** Tape each of the feathers around the back of the mask. Try to alternate the colours.

Ask an adult or friend to help you tape the ends of the card strip together at the back. Add a centrepiece, as shown, if you like.

**5** Cut out a card strip long enough to go around your head with an overlap of 1 inch (2 centimetres). Glue headdress to the strip.

### Did you know?

The Aztecs got brightly coloured feathers from hunters who lived in the rainforests.
The best feathers, from the blue-green quetzal bird, were more valuable than gold.

# Abstract art

You don't have to make your paintings look realistic if you don't want to. Many famous artists painted what they saw using flat patterns, bright colours and interesting shapes. This is called **abstract** art.

**You will need:**
- Paper
- A pencil
- Poster paints
- Brushes
- White glue
- Coloured paper

### Different styles

Many artists moved away from realistic painting and developed styles of their own. **Pablo Picasso** often used a style called cubism, where everything is made of squares. **Henri Matisse** made images with blocks of colour.

'L'Escargot' (The Snail) by Henri Matisse

### Top tip
Henri Matisse often used torn and cut paper to make bold collage images. Try making a collage of your artwork, using pieces of coloured paper instead of paint.

# Make an abstract painting

Decide what you are going to paint – for example, the view from your window, a scene from a postcard, a person or an animal.

**1** Lightly sketch the main parts of the picture with a pencil. Just draw the houses and trees as simple shapes. In this painting, the artist hasn't tried to put anything in the right place – he has just used them to make a pattern of shapes and colours.

**2** Paint the finished picture, using bold colours. Apply the paint in bold blocks of colour, without shading.

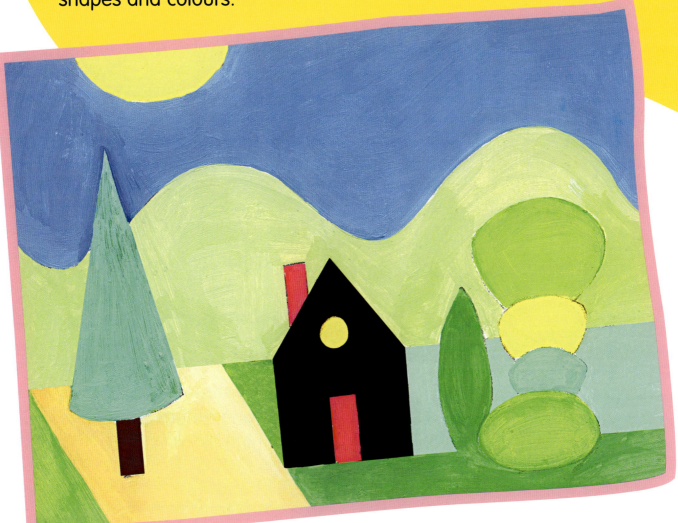

# Painting patterns

Flowers, berries and leaves make great patterns. Look for examples in your garden or local park. Look through magazines, wallpaper samples and fabric remnants to see how artists use natural forms in their designs. You can also make your own natural patterns.

### You will need:
- Pencil
- Thick paper
- Poster paints
- Scissors
- Glue
- Collection of leaves, petals or twigs

## Design your own wallpaper or material

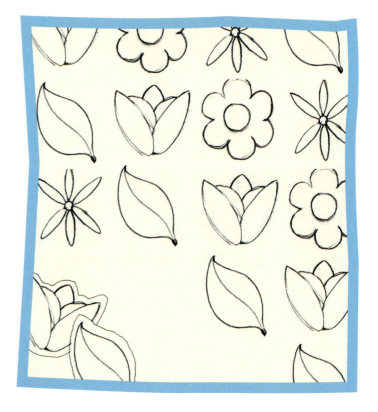

**1** Look through your collection of leaves, flowers and plants and sketch some of your favourite shapes.

**2** Put the shapes together to make a pattern – cut them up and arrange them on the page, glue them in place.

**3** For a repeat design, draw a grid with a pencil and ruler. This will help you to keep the shapes straight, the same size and in the right place. Your shapes can be realistic or imaginative.

**4** Paint the pattern using poster paint. Which works best – two or three colours, or more? Why not try some different designs?

### Top tip
English Victorian artists often used nature in their designs. William Morris used plants, flowers and birds in wallpaper, tapestries, stained-glass windows, tiles and **embroidery**.

81

# Dragging and combing

**You will need:**
- Thick paint
- A wide brush
- Posterboard
- Pieces of cardboard or plastic packaging
- Scissors
- Glue

Dragging and combing pictures and designs in thick, wet paint is a fun way to create images

**1** Cut comb shapes out of cardboard. Make some with thick teeth, and some with small teeth.

**2** Brush a thick coat of paint onto the paper in different colours. Divide the page into roughly equal bands of colour.

**3** While the paint is still wet, drag your card combs through the paint to make waves and lines. The colours will carry over into the other bands, and in some places you will see the paper beneath.

# Scraper art

As well as making patterns, you can use your scrapers to make a picture.

**❶** Paint a wide band of yellow across the bottom of the paper and fill in the rest of the page with blue paint. While the paint is still wet, use a cardboard comb to make swirly waves in the sea. Use a comb to make horizontal lines across the sand, then comb upwards for a **checked** effect.

**❷** On a separate piece of paper, use paint and combs to make sea animals and plants.

**❸** When these are dry, cut them out and glue them to the sea and sand background.

**Add details like the eye on the fish using a felt-tip when your painting is dry.**

83

# Watercolour art

You can get some wonderful effects if you brush watery paint onto wet paper. The colours blend together, giving a very soft result.

**You will need:**
- Watercolour paint
- Soft wide brush
- Thick paper
- Jam jar for water

## Two-colour painting

Practise using two colours to make watery paintings.

**1** Use a wide, soft brush to wet the paper. Then paint a wide strip of yellow across the bottom half of the paper.

**2** Before it dries, dip your brush in the second colour. Brush this gently over the top so that the two colours merge softly. Work quickly before the paint dries!

### Top tip
If you don't want your paintings to go crinkly when they dry, stretch the paper first. Dip the paper very quickly in water, and tape it to a board or piece of cardboard. Once dry, it is ready to use.

# Paint a sunset

**1** Brush water all over the paper with a wide, soft brush. Paint the background in yellow and, while the paint is wet, add some orange streaks.

**2** Now use some dark blue paint to add a band at the top of the image. Let this dry before using white paint to add the sun and its reflection in the water.

**3** Use black paint to make the strip of land about three-quarters of the way up the picture. Add some ripples in light blue in the foreground.

**4** When the paint is dry, use a small brush and dry black paint to add the boats. They appear as silhouettes in the sunset, with dark reflections in the water.

85

# Spatter art

Some artists don't use brushes to paint objects, they just throw the paint onto their pictures! It is a great way of making a fun, lively image with lots of colour.

**You will need:**
- Lots of old newspaper
- A piece of paper
- Paint
- Brushes
- An old toothbrush
- Cardboard

## Make your own messy masterpiece

**1** Cover the floor with newspaper and wear an apron or artist's smock. Put your sheet of paper in the middle.

**2** Flick runny paint onto the paper with brushes. Dip the toothbrush into paint, and run the cardboard over the bristles while you point it at the paper.

**3** Add blobs, drizzles and splats of different colour, until you like the result. Leave some white background showing through.

# Splatter stencils

Spattering over a stencil makes a sharp image on a messy backgrounds.

**1** Cut some shapes out of cardboard. Arrange them on a piece of paper.

**2** Spatter the paint over the paper as before. Carefully lift up the shapes when you have finished.

## Top tip

If you want to make one or more areas of your picture darker, dip a toothbrush in paint then hold it near the area you want to make darker and keep flicking the paint at the paper using your thumb.

# Going BIG!

Choose strong, simple images for a large painting or mural. The trick is to plan them first of all on a sheet of paper. Then its easy to scale them up in size.

**You will need:**
- A4 paper
- A large piece of paper
- Ruler
- Pencil
- Paint
- Brushes

## Using a grid to scale up

**1** Sketch out your drawing or design on a standard sheet of paper. Paint in the colours you want to use.

**2** When the paint has dried, draw a square using a ruler and pencil around your picture. Mark off 2-inch (5 centimetre) intervals on each side of the square. Join the marks up to make a grid. draw a grid over the painting. If the picture doesn't divide exactly into 2-inch (5 centimetre) squares, make the bottom rows slightly smaller.

### Top tip

If you don't want to spoil your first painting, tape a piece of tracing paper over the top and draw the grid on this.

**3** Now take your big piece of paper, and divide it into a grid with the same number of squares – but this time make the squares much bigger. Copy your picture, square by square, in pencil. When you are happy with it, paint it. Use your small painting as a guide to get the colours right.

## Top tip

You can use this technique to create really huge pictures. Lots of different cultures make large images to decorate the walls of their houses or streets. Try making a large image for your classroom wall.

# Body prints

You can make fantastic prints with your hands or fingertips! Just follow these easy steps.

**Top tip**
Keep a bowl of soapy water and a towel handy. Clean your fingers before you dip them in a new colour.

## Butterfly frieze

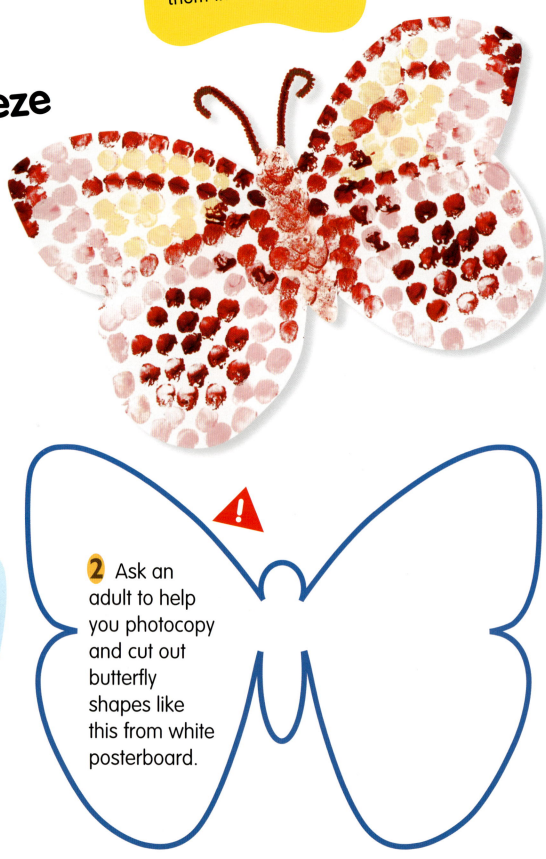

**1** Paint green grass and blue sky on a large sheet of paper and leave it to dry.

**You will need:**
- A large sheet of white paper
- Some white posterboard
- Felt-tip pen or pipe cleaners

**2** Ask an adult to help you photocopy and cut out butterfly shapes like this from white posterboard.

# Apple prints

**1** Paint your palm with red paint and press it onto paper.

**2** Make a brown stalk by printing with the side of a short piece of cardboard.

**3** Press your thumb into green paint to print some leaves.

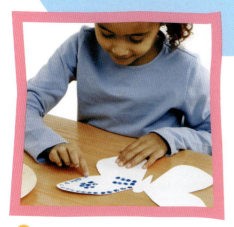

**3** Dip your fingertips in paint and press them onto the cut-out butterfly shapes.

Use your fingertips to print these fun animals, then add details with a felt-tip pen.

**4** Glue the shapes onto the background. Draw feelers with a felt-tip pen, or glue on pipe cleaners.

**Click for Art!** To see ancient handprints on cave walls in Australia, go to www.dvc.vic.gov.au/aav/heritage/mini-posters/14RockArt.pdf

# Leaf prints

This project shows you how to make a printed leaf border for a picture or poem.

**Top tips**
- Make a test print on scratch paper first.
- Leave one colour to dry before you add the next.

**1** To make the border, draw a straight line 2½ inches (6 centimetres) in from each side of your sheet of construction paper or posterboard. Ask an adult to cut out the middle section for you.

**2** Paint the underside of a leaf and press it onto the frame in one corner.

**3** Use the same leaf to make prints in the other corners. Coat the leaf with fresh paint each time.

When your border is dry, glue your picture or poem behind it or use it as a photo frame.

# Nature prints

**You will need:**
- A selection of clean, dry leaves
- Construction paper or posterboard 10 x 12 inches (25 x 30 centimetres)
- Poster paints
- A brush

**4** Build up a **pattern** of leaf shapes in different colours all around the frame. Try beech, sycamore and oak leaves.

Try making prints with:
★ twigs and bark
★ flowers
★ the underside of a mushroom

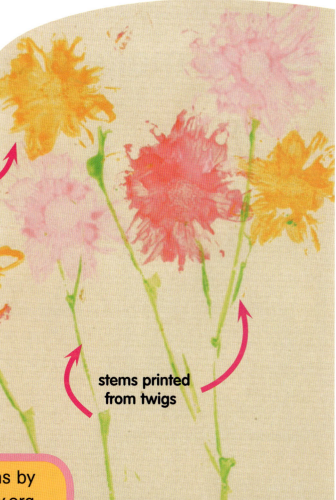

flowers printed from a real flower head

stems printed from twigs

**Click for Art!** To see leaf designs by William Morris, visit www.morrissociety.org Click on the designs and follow the links.

# Junk prints

Pieces of junk, such as nails, screws, cardboard or thread spools make great prints. But always ask before you use them!

Here are some things to try:
★ Corrugated cardboard
★ An empty toilet-paper roll
★ A scrunched-up paper bag
★ Nails, screws or washers
★ An old sponge or cork
★ A Lego® brick or puzzle piece

Racy rocket

plastic bottlecap
corrugated cardboard
screw heads

## How to make a printing pad

Printing pads use less paint and make a clearer, cleaner print.

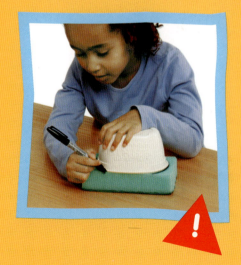

**Top tip**
Don't forget that you will need to make a separate pad for each colour.

**1** Ask an adult to help you cut a piece of foam to fit in the bottom of a plastic bowl. The easiest way is to place the bowl on top of the foam and draw around it first.

**2** Put the foam into the bottom of the bowl and pour over enough paint to cover it. Leave it until the foam soaks up the paint.

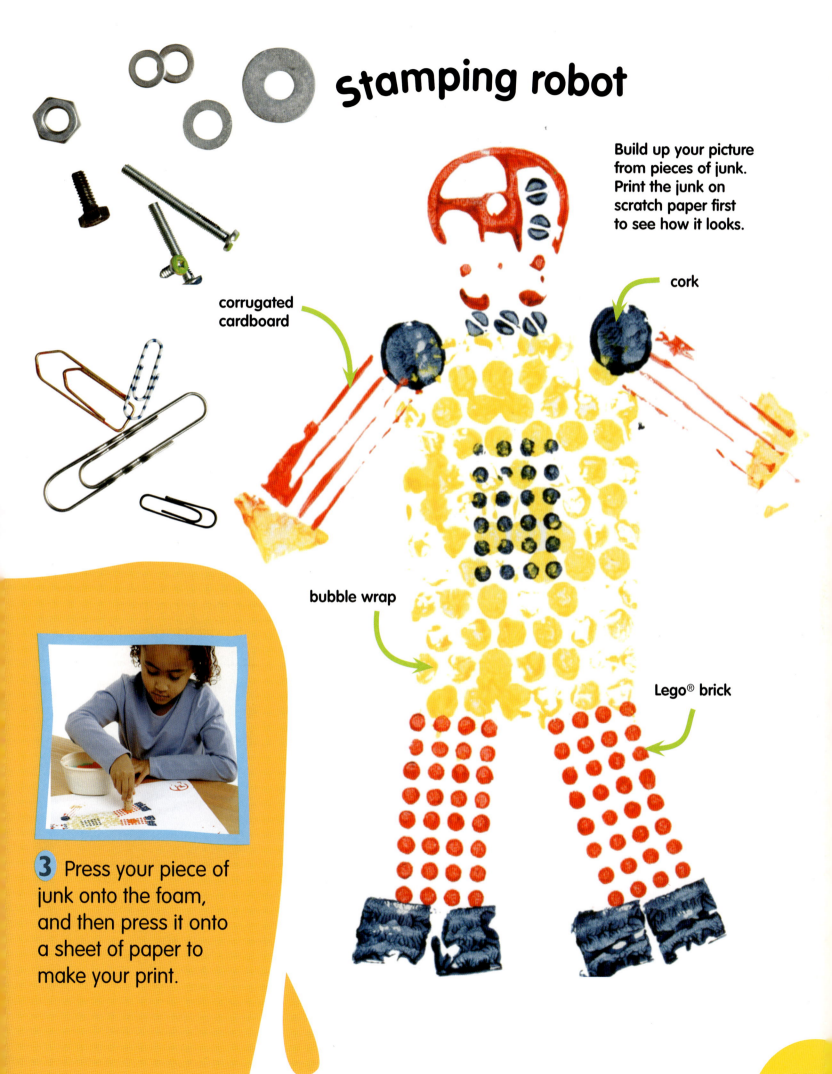

# stamping robot

Build up your picture from pieces of junk. Print the junk on scratch paper first to see how it looks.

cork

corrugated cardboard

bubble wrap

Lego® brick

3 Press your piece of junk onto the foam, and then press it onto a sheet of paper to make your print.

95

# Food prints

Print with fruit or vegetables onto fabric to make fun placemats. Ask an adult to help you with cutting and slicing your food.

**You will need:**
- Food for printing
- Fabric paints
- Pinking shears
- Plain muslin cloth
- A brush

### Food shapes and patterns

Look for food with interesting **patterns** or shapes:

★ Dried pasta shapes, such as wheels, long tubes or butterflies
★ A piece of broccoli or cauliflower
★ Half an apple or orange
★ A large cabbage leaf
★ A slice of carrot or celery
★ Half a red pepper

**1** Set out the food you are going to print with and some dishes of fabric paint. Sketch your rough design on scratch paper first.

**2** Ask an adult to help you cut the fabric for the placemats into rectangles 12 x 10 inches (30 x 25 centimetres). Use pinking shears so the edges do not fray.

### Fabric paints
- Be sure to let each colour dry before you add an overlapping one.
- Most fabric paints need pressing with a hot iron to stop the colours from washing out. Ask an adult to do this for you.

**Click for Art!**

To learn all about traditional block printing on fabric in India, go to www.sashaworld.com/block/block.htm

### Top tip
Wipe the cut surface of fruit or vegetables dry before you paint it. This helps the paint stick better and you will make a clearer print.

**3** Dip the food into the paint, or paint the surface of the food with a brush. Press down firmly on the cloth to make the print.

# Make an Aztec serpent stamp

Snakes were a symbol of the Aztec god Quetzalcoatl (Keht-tsal-coh-ah-tl). His name means 'feathered serpent'.

An Aztec pendant shaped like a two-headed poisonous snake. It is made of turquoise (a semi-precious stone) with carved shells for teeth.

### You will need:
- Two rectangles of cardboard
- Pencil
- Tracing paper
- Craft knife
- Glue
- White, green and blue acrylic paint
- Saucer
- Paintbrush or roller
- Fine paintbrush
- White paper

An Aztec man (right) and woman (left) say prayers in front of a holy statue. This picture was painted 500 years after the Aztecs lived, but shows us what they looked like.

### Did you know?
The Aztecs' own name for themselves was the 'Mexica'. Today, we still use this name for their homeland, Mexico.

**1** Trace the two-headed snake onto one of the cardboard rectangles. Ask an adult to cut it out with a craft knife.

**2** To make your stamp, glue the snake shape to the other card rectangle. Leave to dry completely.

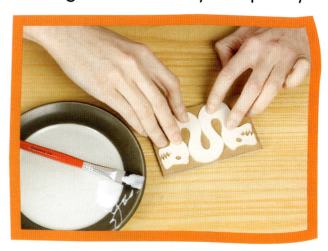

**3** Mix up some turquoise paint. Roll or brush paint evenly over the snake shape on your stamp.

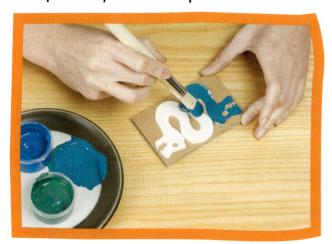

**4** Turn the block over and press down firmly onto white paper. Gently peel away the card to reveal the snake.

**5** Let your snake image dry, then add highlights, such as the eyes, with white paint and a fine paintbrush.

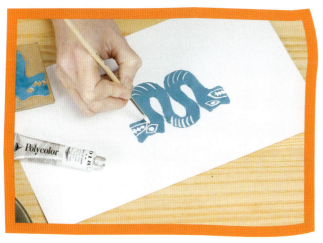

**You can use your stamp over and over again!**

# String prints

Make simple printing blocks by gluing string to small pieces of cardboard or wood. The results are amazing!

**You will need:**
- Paper or posterboard
- A piece of wood, cardboard or a piece of styrofoam for the block
- String
- Poster paints
- A brush

**1** Paint a blue watery background onto paper or posterboard.

**2** When the paint is dry, print tall green reeds with the edge of a long piece of cardboard.

**Top tip**
Sprinkle a little salt onto the blue paint while wet. This will give the background an interesting grainy texture.

**3** Glue string to the printing block in a fish shape. Make a large fish block and a smaller one.

100

**4** Glue on string for the fish's scales. Make an eye from string glued in a spiral or a circle of foam.

**5** Paint the printing block and press onto the background. Paint the block each time you print.

# Simple blocks

You can glue all kinds of things to wood or cardboard to make printing blocks:
★ Grains of rice
★ Nails or screws
★ Buttons
★ A feather
★ Paperclips
★ An old key

**Print fish swimming in the same direction like real fish.**

**Print reeds behind and on top of the fish, so the fish appear to be swimming through them.**

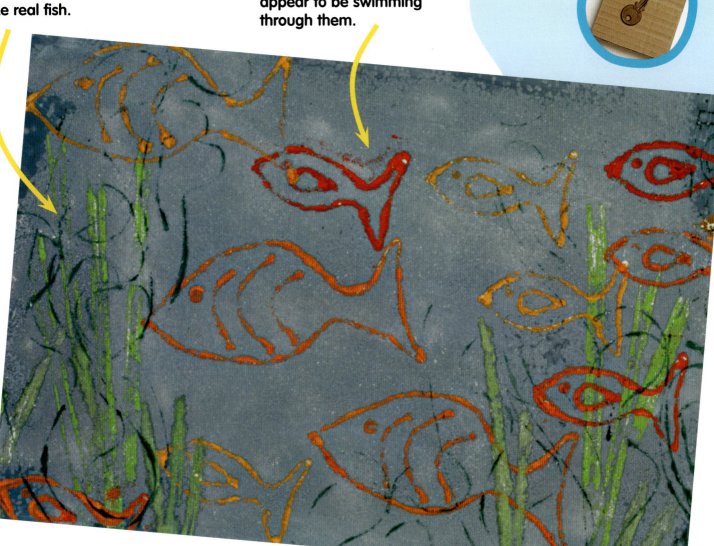

101

# Stencil prints

Cards decorated with stencils are easy to make – and fun to send to your friends!

**You will need:**
- Plain and coloured cardboard
- Thin card for the stencil
- A thick paintbrush
- Poster paints

**1** Choose a shape that is **symmetrical** – the same on both sides.

**2** Fold a small square of cardboard in half. Draw half the design at the fold.

**3** Carefully cut out your stencil and open it out.

**4** Fold a sheet of coloured cardboard in half lengthwise.

**5** Hold your stencil firmly over the front of the card and dab paint through the stencil with a thick, bristly brush.

**Top tip**
Use a little paint at a time so it does not leak under the stencil.

# Wrapping paper and gift tags

Print stencils in a regular pattern onto plain paper to make a sheet of wrapping paper.

Print a stencil onto a square of cardboard and hole-punch it to make a matching gift tag.

**Click for Art!**

To see stencils by Yoshitoshi Mori, go to www.castlefinearts.com/catalog.aspx?catID=97

# Marbling

In marbling, a beautiful print is made from swirling oil paint dripped into water. Oil and water do not mix, so the oil paint stays on the surface of the water and sticks to the paper when it is gently laid on top.

**You will need:**
- A large shallow bowl or tray (such as an old plastic bowl or a baking pan)
- Oil paints and **mineral spirits**
- Pencil, stick or straw
- Heavyweight white paper

1 Fill your bowl or pan almost to the top with water.

2 With an adult, mix the paint with mineral spirits until the paint is runny.

### Top tip
When marbling, use just two colours to start with. If you use too many, they will mix together and become muddy.

# Marbled collage

Cut shapes of marbled paper and stick them onto a background of different-coloured paper so the pictures stand out.

**3** Drop tiny blobs of paint onto the water's surface and gently swirl the colours around with a pencil or a stick.

**4** Lay your paper on the water's surface. Make sure there are no air bubbles trapped underneath the paper.

### Top tip
Instead of stirring the paint with a pencil, try blowing it around the bowl through a straw.

**5** Leave for a few seconds, then gently remove the paper. Place the marbled paper on a flat surface to dry.

**Click for Art!** To see beautiful examples of marbled paper, go to **http://members.aol.com/marbling/marbling**. Click on '28 Examples of marbling'.

# Mirror printing

This is one of the simplest and quickest ways to print. The method is always the same, but every print is different.

**You will need:**
- Poster paints
- Paper
- A brush

## Easy butterfly print

1. Fold the paper in half. Open it out and paint some thick blobs on one side, roughly in the shape of half a butterfly. Make sure the paint goes right into the fold, but not over it.

2. Fold the paper over. Press down firmly, and then open it up.

### Top tip
This works well for **symmetrical** shapes, such as flowers or leaves. See how many designs you can come up with.

**Top tip**
Experiment with string of different thicknesses and texture.

# String prints

String prints make fascinating, swirly patterns.

**You will need:**
- Paper
- Poster paints
- Saucers
- String
- Scissors

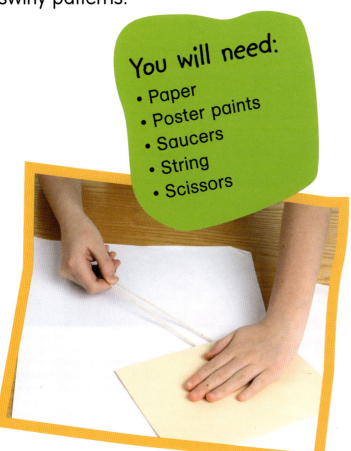

**1** Cut three lengths of string. Put three different-coloured poster paints into separate saucers. Put a piece of string in each saucer. Make sure the strings are well coated with paint.

**2** Fold a piece of paper in half, then open it back out, as you did for the mirror print. Lay the strings carefully on one side of the paper, with one end of each string sticking out over the edge.

**3** Fold the other half of the paper over again and press your hand firmly over the surface. Keeping your hand pressed down, pull out the strings by their ends. Open the paper to see your swirly string picture!

# Printing from card

One of the most common methods of printing is to use blocks. These can be complicated or very simple. You can make your own blocks for printing – the easiest are simple shapes cut out of cardboard.

### Print kit
Save as many different types of cardboard as possible – **corrugated** is great for stripy, textured prints. You can use all parts of the cardboard – the smooth sides are good for printing blocks of colour, while the edges are useful for lines and curves. Use the ends of straws or cardboard tubes to make circles or ovals.

### Top tip
To make your blocks easier to use, glue a small piece of cork or Styrofoam to the back to serve as a handle.

### Print a greetings card
Try making blocks for a simple greeting card. You can reuse them to make a batch of cards – perfect for Christmas.

You will need:
- Poster paints
- A brush
- Cardboard and paper
- Scissors

1 Sketch out your ideas for the card design on scrap paper. Keep the shapes simple.

**2** Now cut out the shapes you need for your design. You can glue small pieces of Styrofoam to the back to serve as handles.

**3** Brush the largest printing block with paint. Then press it firmly onto the paper and peel it off to reveal the print beneath.

**4** When the first colour is dry, do the same with the smaller blocks until your picture is finished. Try not to smudge!

**5** You can add details by printing with the top of pen lids.

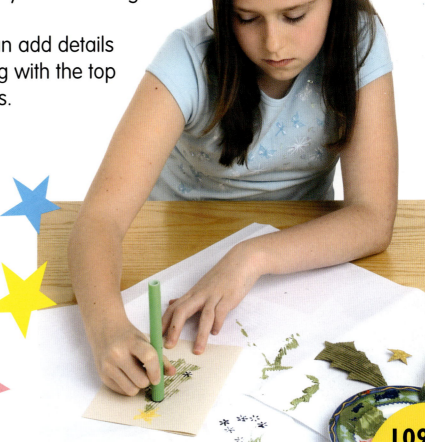

### Top tip
Remember when you make a print that the finished print will be a mirror image of your printing block!

109

# Making blocks

By gluing objects to small pieces of wood, you can make printing blocks that you can reuse over and over again. See what objects you can find around the house, to add to your printing blocks.

### Simple kit
Glue string to small pieces of wood or heavyweight cardboard in interesting shapes for simple prints.

Try making shapes from foam, rubber, sponge, old keys, paper clips, dried pasta, buttons, buckles, old toys or broken jewellery. Almost anything will work!

**You can paint on lots of bright colours to get a rainbow effect.**

**Let your imagination run wild – but don't forget to ask permission first.**

### Make a bookplate
Glue string onto one side of a block of wood to form the shape of your initial (remember to do it in reversed mirror writing). Add a few decorations, and use it to print your initial in the front page of your books. You could also use it to make headed notepaper.

# Sponge stamps

**You will need:**
- A sponge
- A craft knife
- A brush
- Poster paint
- Paper

These are ideal for crisp, clean prints. They are expensive to buy – but you can make your own.

**1** Draw a simple design on the soft side of the sponge.

**2** Ask an adult to cut away the parts around the design using a craft knife.

**3** Brush or roll paint over the raised surface and then press the stamp down onto the paper.

Sponges are also great for smaller patterns, such as wallpaper for a dolls' house. You could even print your own 'postage stamps'.

Try printing a trail of animal tracks. Glue thin stamps around the outside of a stiff cardboard tube, and use it as a roller printer.

# Prints from nature

Some of the most delicate prints are made from objects from the natural world. Feathers, leaves, flowers and wood all make intricate prints. Using prints, you can make a pattern that would take hours to paint with a brush.

**Print kit**

See what natural printers you can find when you are out on a walk. Some, such as feathers and bark, will keep more or less forever, while green leaves will have to be used before they dry out.

Roll or brush poster paint carefully over leaves, ferns, wheatstalks, etc., and press them onto paper to make a print. Experiment with different effects and colours. For example, a white leaf or fern print looks great on dark paper.

### Top tip

Leaves don't last very long, but you can make long-lasting leaf-shaped printers! Just trace around leaves onto heavyweight cardboard, cut them out and use them as printing blocks.

# Leaf prints

Choose three different types of leaf and brush each one with different colour of paint to print a pattern.

**You will need:**
- A collection of leaves – at least three different types
- Bright poster paint
- Paper
- A brush

**1** Brush a bright colour over one of the leaves, and press it down onto dark-coloured paper. Do this several times, then let the paint dry.

**2** Take a different leaf, and use a different coloured paint. Print onto the paper, overlapping the first leaf prints.

**3** Continue printing, until hardly any of the dark background shows through.

**Mount your picture on coloured paper and place it on your wall.**

### Top tip
Try printing while the first colour is still wet. Use pastel colours on white paper for an airy, delicate effect.

# Potato prints

A potato print is a cross between a printing with food and a block.

**Print kit**

All you need to make a potato printer is a big potato and a craft knife. Your printer won't last very long, but if you slice off the old design, you can start again on the fresh surface. Other 'root' vegetables make good printing blocks, too – try a few and see which ones work best.

**You will need:**
- A large potato
- A sharp pencil
- A craft knife
- Poster paints
- Paper

**1** Ask an adult to cut the potato in half. Draw a simple design on the cut surface with a sharp pencil. Try a butterfly, a flower or a star.

**2** Ask the adult to cut around the design and remove the excess from the edges so your design sticks out. Brush paint over the surface of the design.

**3** Press the painted surface firmly onto paper. Rock the printer gently, so that all parts of the design touch the paper.

**Try coloured paper and contrasting paints for attractive wrapping paper.**

Your friends and family will much prefer a hand-made gift tag with your own design on it.

## Top tip
It's fun to make your own gift tags. Cut lots of small rectangles from coloured cardboard and fold them in half. Punch a hole in the top-left corner to thread some ribbon through. Then use potato printers to make a design. You could make an interesting border around the edges, too.

## Top tip
Use a biscuit cutter to make an instant printer! Just press the cutter into a potato, and ask an adult to cut away around the outside before removing the cutter.

## Top tip
Try using different coloured paints on different parts of a butterfly to get some really interesting, multi-coloured results!

# Make a Pop Art print

The artist **Andy Warhol** often repeated the same image several times over to make bold, bright paintings and prints. Here's how to make a really striking Pop Art print, Warhol-style, for your wall.

You will need:
- A ruler and pencil
- Bright poster paints
- Bubble wrap
- Black felt-tip pen
- A simple printer – this could be a cardboard or wooden block, a potato or a piece of fruit
- Thick cardboard
- Brushes
- **Polyvinyl white glue**

**1** Brush brightly coloured paint over the bubble wrap, and press it down onto the paper to print a dotty pattern. Do this several times, and use a different colour for each piece of paper. Use the ruler and pencil to cut the prints into neat squares, each the same size.

**2** Glue the squares to a piece of cardboard to make a **checkered** effect. Leave a wide border. Brush paint over your printer and press it onto the first square – choose a colour that contrasts with the dots. Red and green, blue and orange and yellow and purple all make good contrasts.

**3** Carry on printing onto the squares until every one is filled. Use the black felt-tip pen to go over the lines of each square. Cut some cardboard to make a frame. Paint it in a bright colour and then cut a wavy outline with scissors. Tape a loop of yarn to the back so that you can hang it up.

**The dots in your picture will make it look like the prints that Andy Warhol made.**

## Make a pop art notebook

Protect the print with adhesive plastic. Place an open notebook on the back of the print, and draw around it. Draw a border of 2 inches (5 centimetres). Cut flaps in the border, and fold them over the covers of the book, gluing them in place. Glue the first and last pages of the notebook to the covers, to hide the flaps.

# Monoprints

A monoprint is made by pressing a piece of paper over a painted design, and lifting it off. The textures and shapes you get would be impossible to create by painting – they may not always be successful, but when they are, they can be brilliant!

### Print kit
You will need a really smooth surface to print from – a piece of formica, a mirror, or a shiny baking sheet are ideal. Water-based printing inks give the best effects, but you can also use thick paint. Mix the paint with a little dishwashing detergent and white glue to keep it from drying out too quickly. As with the mirror prints on page 106, a monoprint (meaning 'one print') can never be repeated.

### Top tip
When you roll your paint out onto the flat surface, try mixing two colours together to create an interesting graduation between one colour and the next. Experiment with multi-coloured monoprints, using lots of different colours.

### Take Care !
Be careful if you are using glass to print on – you will need adult help. Check with an adult before you use a table or other piece of furniture to make your monoprint.

# Drawing a monoprint

In this project, you draw a shape to create a monoprint beneath.

**You will need:**
- Thick paint or printing ink
- A smooth surface
- A roller or wide brush
- Paper

**1** Roll bands of colour onto the smooth surface, and place the paper lightly on top.

**2** Using a pencil, crayon or knitting needle, draw a design on the paper – try to press the paper just on the lines you are drawing.

**3** Lift up the paper gently, making sure not smudge the image. Let it dry out completely.

# Stencils

Stenciling was very popular among the early pioneers, who couldn't buy wallpaper or decorated furniture. Practise stenciling on paper or cardboard first – when you feel confident enough, you could use the stencils to decorate your bedroom.

**what you need:**
- Rigid stencil paper or thin cardboard
- A short-haired brush
- Thick paint
- A pencil
- A craft knife
- Paper

### Print kit

There are plenty of pre-made stencils to use for printing. You can also buy stencils from craft shops. You will need a brush with short, stubby bristles to make stencils. The paint should be almost dry, and you should dab it over the stencil. This technique is called 'stippling'.

**1** Draw a simple design onto stencil paper or cardboard with a pencil.

**2** Ask an adult to cut out the shape with a craft knife.

**3** Tape the stencil to the sheet of paper. Using an almost dry brush, stipple the paint over the hole in the stencil, making sure that you go right up to the edges.

**Stencil spatter**

Instead of stippling your stencil design, you can spatter! Just load the paint onto an old toothbrush, point the brush at the paper, and run cardboard over the bristles. Use interesting shapes such as leaves, keys or tools. What happens if you move them slightly, and then spatter again with another colour?

### Top tip
Use a simple stenciled design to decorate writing paper and matching envelopes. You could also make stencil wrapping paper – use spray paint for really quick results.

# Spray stenciling

For really quick stenciling, you could use spray paint. Spray paints come in lots of interesting colours, such as silver – as used here.

### Top tip !
You can use your stencils to decorate lots of personal belongings. Ask an adult for help with cutting.

**1** Make a large stencil with a repeat pattern. Place it over coloured paper and spray paint over it.

**2** Make sure you cover each part of the stencil, and then lift the stencil off Let it dry for a few minutes.

121

# Printing pictures

The more you experiment with different kinds of printers, the more ideas you are likely to get for your pictures. You can mix prints with **collage** and paint effects, too. Try to think about your prints in a new way – a cabbage leaf print may look just like a cabbage leaf – but it would also make a great tree!

**You will need:**
- Cabbage leaves
- Thick paints
- Thin, watered-down paints
- Brushes
- Paper
- Thick paper
- White glue
- Scissors

## Trees in the park

In this project, you can use cabbage leaves to create intricate tree shapes that would take a long time to draw or paint.

**1** Paint the background very quickly, using a wide, soft brush and thin, watered-down paints. Let it dry (taping it down to your work surface prevents the paper from wrinkling).

**2** Now make lots of tree prints, using cabbage leaves of different sizes. Use a good variety of colours, from yellow-green to greens with a brown or bluish shade.

A stippling brush (one with short, stiff bristles) is good for brushing paint onto the cabbage leaf.

**3** When the 'trees' are dry, cut them out and glue them to the picture. Finish the picture by printing the fence, using the edge of a piece of cardboard brushed with brown paint.

Can you make a print collage like this of your favourite view? Or what about a fantasy landscape – such as a spaceship landing on a distant planet?

### Top tip
Cauliflower and broccoli make good trees, too. Simple shapes torn from paper make delicate clouds, misty mountains, icebergs or rough rocks. Sandpaper is perfect for cliffs.

# Materials kit

This section will show you how to make amazing crafts from around the world. On this page you can see most of the things you need to get going. Some extras are listed with each project.

1. Sticky tape or masking tape
2. Paper glue
3. Dish of wallpaper paste for papier-mâché projects
4. Balloons
5. Paintbrushes
6. Paper fasteners
7. Poster paints
8. Air-drying modelling clay
9. Enamel paint
10. Beads, stick-on gems, sequins, etc.
11. Coloured paper
12. Paint roller
13. Crayons and coloured chalk
14. Pencils
15. Ruler
16. Safety scissors
17. String
18. Tissue paper
19. Sketch pad
20. Cutting board

## Paints and paintbrushes

As well as different coloured poster paint, you will need some white latex paint for first coats on clay or papier-mâché models. You also need a selection of paintbrushes: a small decorating brush (for glue or to paint large areas), a medium-sized brush, and a thin brush for fine detail.

### Take care!

For some projects in this book you will need help from an adult; when using a craft knife or hammer and nails, for example. The instructions will tell you when you need to ask for help.

## Craft foam

Craft foam is useful for all kinds of craft projects. You can buy sheets of brightly coloured craft foam. Some craft shops also sell bags of pre-cut foam squares and shapes.

### Dangerous stuff!

Most wallpaper paste contains a **fungicide**, which is poisonous and may cause an allergic reaction in some people. Before you use it, dab a dot of paste on the inside of your wrist and leave it for a few minutes. If your skin becomes irritated, do not use it, or wear thin plastic gloves. Never get wallpaper paste in your eyes, nose or mouth and always wash your hands well after use.

125

# African cloth picture

In Benin, Africa, people tell stories in brightly coloured cloth pictures. You can make your own picture using **felt**.

**A long time ago, cloth pictures like these hung behind the throne of the king of Benin.**

### You will need:
- Felt (black, red, yellow, orange)

**Ask an adult to help you enlarge these animal shapes on a photocopier.**

**1** Draw an animal with felt-tip pen on the back of a piece of felt. Ask an adult to help you cut it.

**Click for Art!**

To see traditional cloth pictures from Benin, visit www.kidstoafrika.org/benin/tapestries

**Top tip**
Cut scraps of different-coloured felt and glue them onto your animal shape.

**2** Ask an adult to help you cut out a piece of black felt for your background. Make it at least 2 inches (5 centimetres) bigger than your felt shape.

**3** Cut out four strips of coloured felt 1 inches (3 centimetres) wide to make a frame. Overlap the strips at each corner and glue them in place.

**4** Glue your animal picture in the middle of the black background.

# Egyptian collar

Neck collars were made from semiprecious stones or gold, clay or glass beads. How many pretty bits and pieces can you find for yours?

**Did you know?**
Many Egyptian children wore no clothes at all until they were old enough to marry, at around 12 years old. Some servants also went naked.

Queen Nefertari, dressed in a tight, patterned robe, fashionable around 1500 B.C.E. She also wears thick eyeliner, a heavy jewelled collar and bracelets on both arms.

Put your collar on and tie at the back. For a real Egyptian look, you could add a thin headband!

128

## You will need:
- 16 x 16 inchches (40 x 40 centimetre) square of felt
- Compass
- Scissors
- Glue
- Beads, gems, buttons, sequins, felt scraps
- Red ribbon

**1** Set your compass to 5 inches (12 centimetres) and draw a circle. Set it to 1 1/2 inches (4 centimetres). Draw another from the same point.

**2** Cut both circles out. Then cut away a small section of the collar shape, as shown here.

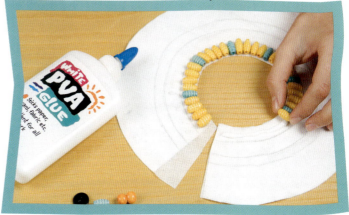

**3** Put a line of glue around the inside of the collar and place different-coloured beads along it.

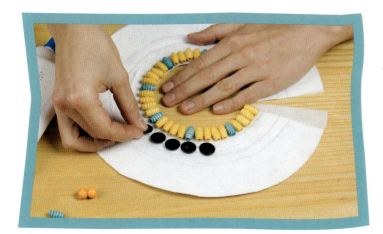

**4** Add another line of glue and more buttons. In this way, continue to build up the pattern.

**5** On each side of the collar, glue one end of a length of red ribbon to the felt backing.

# Roman robe clasp

Romans did not have zips or buttons. They used clasps and brooches instead. Make a stunning dog clasp for your Roman robe!

This dog-shaped brooch was used to fasten a Roman robe. It is made of bronze and decorated with enamel (coloured glass).

### Did you know?
Roman women wore wigs! The wigs were made from dark hair purchased from India or from blonde hair cut from German captives and slaves.

### You will need:
- Pencil
- Tracing paper
- White pencil
- Black cardstock
- Scraps of gold foil
- Scissors
- Glue
- Coloured paper
- Gold pen
- Safety pin
- Tape
- Black fine-tip marker

Roman women wore their long hair arranged in many complicated styles. Roman men were clean shaven with short hair, except around 100–200 C.E., when they preferred longer curls and beards.

**1** Draw or trace the dog shape onto black cardstock and go over it in white pencil. Cut it out with scissors.

**2** Draw the body shape and eye on gold foil and cut out. Now glue them onto your black dog shape.

**3** Cut out small shapes from coloured paper. Arrange and then glue them onto the gold panel.

**4** Use a gold pen to add teeth, a collar, and details to the ears and legs. Draw a solid black circle on the eye.

**5** Use a small piece of masking tape to attach a safety pin to the back of your cloak clasp.

**Romans used clasps to hold their cloaks together, but you could pin yours to a white sheet worn as a toga.**

131

# Aboriginal painting

This project shows you how to paint a dot picture in the style of the Australian **Aboriginal** people.

**1** Paint the whole paper pale yellow or orange. Leave to dry.

**2** Ask an adult to help you copy the lizard shape below onto your picture. Paint it a rich, rusty red. Add wavy lines around it in dark orange or red and allow to dry.

**3** Dip a cotton swab in white or yellow paint. Print rows of dots on the lizard's back and on some of the wavy lines.

**You will need:**
- Acrylic or poster paints in rich, warm colours
- Cotton swabs

**Click for Art!**

For examples of Aboriginal dot paintings, go to www.thebritishmuseum.ac.uk/compass/ and search on 'Aboriginal art'.

**4** Paint large orange or red circles around the lizard. When the paint is dry, print black or brown and white or red dots on the circles.

Lively dot patterns and warm, earthy colours are typical of Aboriginal art.

### Top tip
Arrange blobs of different-coloured paint in saucers. Use a different cotton swab for each colour.

# Roman laurel leaf crown

Make a laurel leaf crown and dress up as an all-powerful emperor. Remind everyone that the emperor's word is law!

**Laurel leaf crowns were symbols of victory and superhuman power. Emperors and top athletes wore them.**

### You will need:
- Pipe cleaners
- Thin, green cardstock
- Ruler
- Pencil
- Scissors
- Masking tape
- Cardboard
- Thin, turquoise cardstock
- Glue stick

### Did you know?
Emperor Caligula (37–41 C.E.) made his horse Prime Minister. Emperor Nero (54–68 C.E.) set fire to Rome, then sang as he watched it burn.

**Before a Roman feast, slaves helped guests take off their outdoor clothes – and washed their feet!**

**1** Twist four pipe cleaners together in a row. Cut out a ¾ inch (2 centimetre)-wide strip of the same length from green cardstock.

**2** Twist together the ends of the pipe cleaners to make a loop. Use masking tape to attach the strip.

**4** Concertina fold a strip of cardstock. Draw around the template onto it. Cut the shape out, cutting through all the layers.

**3** Draw a leaf onto cardboard and cut it out. This will be your template for step 4.

**Be like a good emperor – honest, wise, and fair.**

**5** Stick each leaf to the crown with glue. Repeat step 4 to make as many leaves as you need to cover the ring.

135

# Roman serpent arm bracelet

Swirling snake bracelets were popular with Roman women. Snakes were a symbol of good health for the woman and her family. They were also painted on walls and added to mosaic floor patterns.

A Roman mother and her children. They came from a rich family. You can see that the girl is wearing beautiful jewels.

### You will need:
- 2 pipe cleaners
- Ruler
- Pencil
- Gold cardstock
- Scissors
- Masking tape
- Glue
- Fine-tip black marker

**1** Twist two pipe cleaners together. Measure the length of the two pipe cleaners.

**2** Draw two rectangles on gold cardstock that are each the same length as the pipe cleaners and 1/2 inch (1.5 centimetres) wide.

**3** Use masking tape to attach the pipe cleaners to the back of one rectangle. Glue the other on top.

**4** Using the black marker, draw a snake's head. Then add the body and swirly tail.

**Wear your serpent on your upper arm like a Roman!**

**5** Curl the snake around your lower arm. When it's the right shape, you can push it to the top of your arm.

137

# Chinese paper dragon

At New Year, Chinese people dance in the street with huge paper and cloth dragons. Here's how to make a puppet dragon.

**You will need:**
- Coloured cardboard or posterboard
- Sequins, glitter, and a 'googly' eye
- Pair of chopsticks or lollipop sticks

**1** Trace the dragon's head and tail onto tracing paper, then onto cardboard. Ask an adult to help you cut out the shapes.

**2** Paint both sides of a sheet of white paper bright red. When dry, fold the paper in half lengthwise and cut along the fold.

**3** Fold the pieces of paper to form an accordion. Glue the two pieces of paper together to make one long piece for the dragon's body.

Ask an adult to enlarge these shapes on a photocopier.

**Click for Art!**
To learn about dragons in Ancient China go to www.chinapage.com/dragon1.html

The dragon dance is performed at Chinese New Year to bring good luck.

plastic 'googly' eye

**4** Paint the dragon's head and tail bright colours and glue on sequins, glitter and a 'googly' eye.

**5** Glue the head and tail to the dragon's body with white craft glue.

**6** Glue the chopsticks or lollipop sticks to the head and tail of the dragon.

# Dye material the Viking way

Vikings used berries and vegetables to dye material beautiful colours. Their dyeing technique still works 1,000 years later!

**You will need:**
- 2 pounds (1 kilogramme) raw beetroot
- Knife
- Cutting board
- Rubber gloves
- Saucepan
- 3.3 feet (1 metre) cotton tape
- White cotton T-shirt
- Wooden spoon
- Colander
- Acrylic paint and paintbrushes
- Double-sided tape

**Did you know?**
Vikings bathed at least once a week – usually on a Saturday – by having a sauna (a bath in clouds of steam). This amazed the English, who washed less often.

This rich Viking man is wearing a cosy fur hat, a thick wool cloak and fur-lined leather boots.

**1** Chop the beetroot and put it in a saucepan half-filled with cold water. Remember to wear rubber gloves.

**2** Put in the tape and T-shirt. Ask an adult to bring it to the boil. Simmer for 1 hour, stirring occasionally.

**3** When cool, strain through a colander. Then, remove the tape and T-shirt from the beetroot pulp.

**4** Rinse well and hang up to drip dry. Once the tape's dry, paint a Viking pattern along it.

**5** When the T-shirt and tape are dry, stick or sew the tape to the T-shirt.

Feel like a proud Viking in your bright, patterned top. (Don't forget that your top is not colourfast and should always be washed separately.)

# Mexican Metapec sun

Mexican craftspeople make beautiful clay pottery. Here's how to make a **Metapec** clay sun to hang on your wall.

### You will need:
- Air-drying clay
- A rolling pin
- A mixing bowl
- A blunt kitchen knife
- Bright acrylic or poster paints
- Paintbrushes
- String or twine

A typical Metapec clay sun from Mexico.

**1** Soften the clay in your hands, then flatten it with a rolling pin. It needs to be about ½ inch (1.5 centimetres) thick and a bit bigger than your mixing bowl.

**2** Place a mixing bowl over the clay. Ask an adult to help you cut around the bowl with a dull knife.

**3** Make holes for the eyes and mouth. Make clay eyes and eyebrows, a nose and mouth, and stick them on with a little water.

### Top tip
To make your sun look happy or surprised, make faces in the mirror and copy how your mouth and eyes change.

 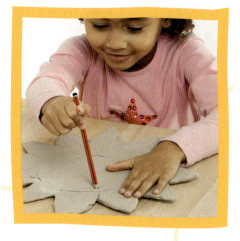

**4** Make clay rays to go around your sun's face. Press them firmly into place or stick them on with a little water.

**5** Push a pencil through the top of the sun to make a hole for the string.

**6** Let your sun harden, then paint it in bright colours. Thread string through the hole at the top so you can hang it on the wall.

### Top tip
To make your clay sun look shiny, paint it with white glue mixed with water. The glue looks white when wet, but will be clear and shiny when it is dry.

# Ancient world art

Many thousands of years ago in the **Stone Age**, people produced some fantastic paintings. Many were made in caves – possibly as decorations for **ceremonies** or on religious **shrines**. Follow the steps below to recreate a magical Stone-Age animal painting.

### You will need:
- Air-drying clay
- Rolling pin
- Sand
- Poster paint
- Black charcoal (optional)
- Cotton balls
- Sandpaper
- Varnish (optional)

**A Stone-Age cave painting**

1. Lightly draw an animal outline, such as a cow, deer, **bison** or elephant on scrap paper. Use a soft pencil and keep the lines simple.

### Top tip
Draw the animal's legs at an angle, not straight down, so it looks as though it is running.

2

**2** Roll out a piece of pale modelling clay (the size of a tennis ball). It doesn't have to be totally smooth. Rub some sand over the clay for a rough surface texture. Then let the clay dry hard.

3

**3** Squirt black and white paint into two separate pools. Mix some to make a light grey, and use cotton wool or a piece of foam to dab it on the clay. When this is dry, paint your animal outline in black.

### Top tip

You can seal your painting with white glue mixed with water instead of varnish. Put some white glue in a plastic cup. Gradually add water until it is the consistency of single cream. It looks white when you paint it on, but it dries clear.

4

**4** Paint the body in natural colours, such as dark browns and reds.

**5** When the paint is dry, gently rub sandpaper over the surface to make it look patchy and old.

**6** Add two coats of clear varnish. Let the varnish dry between coats.

5

6

145

# Aztec mask

This death mask is guaranteed to frighten your friends. Tezcatlipoca was the god of night and the future. Aztecs believed he started wars.

### Did you know?
An ordinary person wishing to speak to a ruler at the palace had to keep their eyes looking down and bow very low. When they left, they walked backwards because it was very rude to face away from the ruler.

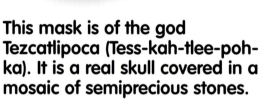

This mask is of the god Tezcatlipoca (Tess-kah-tlee-poh-ka). It is a real skull covered in a mosaic of semiprecious stones.

**No Aztec pyramid temples have survived. But they would have looked like this pyramid, built by earlier Mexican people in the city of Teotihuacan.**

### You will need:
- A piece of black cardstock
- Ruler
- Pencil
- Scissors
- Craft knife
- Silver foil
- Blue, green, turquoise, black and white paper
- Glue
- Elastic thread
- White felt or cardstock

1. Measure your face. On the cardstock, draw an oval shape that is big enough to completely cover your face.

2. Draw on the eyes, mouth and nose. Then ask an adult to cut them out with a craft knife.

3. Glue on two wide strips of foil. Cut out the eyes, nose and mouth holes. Glue on coloured paper shapes.

4. Use a sharp pencil to make holes for the elastic at each side of the mask, below the eyes.

5. Finally, thread elastic through the side holes. Put the mask on. Gently tighten the elastic and knot it to secure the mask.

**Put on your mask and imagine that you can see into the future, like a god.**

# Egyptian amulet

The **Ancient Egyptians** believed that people's spirits must be reunited with their bodies after they died. They decorated dead bodies with amulets, or lucky charms. In this project, you can make a Wedjat-eye charm, which were used by the Egyptians to ward off evil spirits.

You will need:
- Air-drying clay
- Rolling pin or bottle
- Plastic knife
- Wooden or plastic modelling tools
- Poster paint
- Varnish

**1** Roll out a piece of clay, until it is ½ to ¾ inch (1–2 centimetres) thick and about ¾ inches (2 centimetres) larger than you want your finished eye to be. Carve the outline of an eye on the clay with a modelling tool or pencil. Cut out the shape with a plastic knife.

**Ancient Egyptian scarab (beetle) amulets**

**2** Roll out long, thin pieces of clay and press them into the eye shape to build up the design.

**3** Use your tools to make patterns in the clay for decoration.

### Top tip
Everyday household objects, such as a fork, a blunt nail or the end of a paintbrush, make great tools.

**4** When the model is dry, paint it. Once the paint is dry, add a coat of **varnish**. Let this first coat dry and then add another.

### Top tip
To get a smooth surface for decorating, paint an undercoat of white latex paint. Let this dry before adding coloured poster paint.

# Ancient Greek vase

The best pottery in **Ancient Greece** was made in **Athens**. A vase, like the one below, would have stored oil, wine or water. The vase in this project is made of papier-mâché, so don't put liquid in it!

**You will need:**
- Large, oval-shaped balloon
- Newspaper
- Wallpaper paste
- Paint and brushes

**1** Blow up the balloon. Make some wallpaper paste. Tear sheets of newspaper into 1-inch (2½ centimetre) x 2-inch (5 centimetre) strips.

A replica of a vase from Ancient Greece. The pictures show scenes from history and from stories about the gods.

**2** Soak the strips in the paste, then lay them over the balloon neatly so they overlap. Cover the balloon in two layers. Let it dry.

**3** Repeat until you have eight layers. When the paste is dry, pop the balloon with a pin.

**4** Cut out a strip of thin cardboard and tape it in a circle to the base of the balloon shape. Attach a wider piece to the top. Cut two more strips of cardboard and tape them to the sides of the vase for handles.

**5** Cover the cardboard base, top and handles with two layers of strips. Make sure that the strips overlap the main part of the vase. When dry, add another layer.

**6** When this is dry, paint the vase reddish brown. Paint the base, rim, and handles of the vase black.

**7** Draw the owl – the symbol of the goddess **Athena** – onto the side. Paint the owl outline black. Paint decorative borders on the base and top of your vase. When it is dry, varnish the whole vase.

# Roman-style mosaic

Many **Roman** homes had a mosaic – a picture made of tiny glass, stone, or tile squares called 'tesserae' – pressed into the floor. Mosaics showed pictures of many different things.

You will need:
- Graph paper
- Coloured paper or white paper and poster paints, or old magazines, or sticky coloured paper
- Black construction paper
- Scissors
- White glue

**1** Plan your design on graph paper, about 9 x 6 inches (22 ½ x 15 centimetres). Copy this dog mosaic or choose another animal – or your initials. Design a border to frame your design.

**Roman mosaics**

152

### Top tip
Squares cut from magazines give you different **hues** of each of your colours, which gives your design more depth.

**2** Place the paper with the design on it face-down on the construction paper. Rub the paper with the pencil, so the design transfers onto the sugar paper.

**3** Cut equal-size squares from coloured paper. Sort each colour into a separate pile: blues, greens, reds, etc.

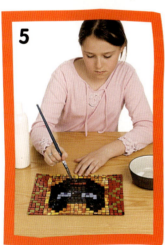

**4** Glue the squares onto the construction paper. Leave a gap about ⅛ inch (3 millimetres) wide between each square.

**5** To make your mosaic shine, paint it with white glue mixed with water.

### Top tip
If you want your mosaic to sparkle, cover some squares in glitter glue or paint them in gold or silver metallic paint.

# Indian Rangoli

Rangoli is the Indian art of decorating the floor or wall with a **geometric** design, flowers or animals. Intricate Rangoli are painted during **Hindu** festivals, such as **Diwali**, or for birthdays. Each state of India has its own style of Rangoli.

You will need:
- Coloured construction paper
- Sketch paper
- Pencil
- White chalk
- Coloured chalk (or flour) with food colouring

1 Practise drawing small Rangoli on sketch paper. Draw a larger version on a big sheet of paper. Start with a series of evenly spaced dots.

An Indian woman making a Rangoli.

**2** Join some of the dots to form a geometric pattern, a flower or animal shape. Here are some ideas.

**3** Copy your design onto the pavement or playground in chalk or in a flour and water paste (always ask permission first); or draw your Rangoli on a large sheet of black construction paper.

### Top tip
Make sure your dots are evenly spaced so that you end up with a regular pattern.

**4** Colour your Rangoli with chalk. If you use flour paste, divide the paste into separate bowls and add a couple of drops of different food colouring to each.

155

# Chinese calligraphy

In China and Japan, calligraphy (beautiful writing produced with a brush) is an art form. Calligraphers spend months practising one character, or symbol. The Chinese character on the card in this project means 'Peace'.

### You will need:
- Paintbrush and paint (optional)
- Pencil
- Black marker pen
- White heavyweight paper
- Cream heavyweight paper
- Dark heavyweight paper
- Red marker pen
- Ruler
- Scissors

**Chinese calligraphy scroll**

1 Draw the outline of the 'Peace' character as shown below, using the graph lines to help you. If you are using a brush, follow the red arrows inside the outlines.

**2** When you have completed the outlines, fill them in with a black marker. Try to keep within your pencil marks.

> **Top tip**
> If you use a brush, try different sizes. A thick, pointed brush makes bold, sweeping strokes. Lift the brush away from the paper to make thin, light brush strokes.

**3** Cut out a rectangle of thick, textured cream paper. Fold in half. To make a neat fold, measure where you want the fold to be with a ruler and mark the line in pencil.

**4** Colour the right edge of the paper in bright red poster paint or marker pen.

**5** Cut a piece of dark paper slightly larger than your calligraphy and stick it to the cream paper. Now glue the calligraphy on top, so that a border of dark paper shows through.

**Here are two other Chinese characters to practise. They mean 'Beautiful' (left) and 'Lucky' (right).**

# Dress up as an Aztec warrior

Warriors wore real jaguar skins to show that they shared the strength and fierceness of a big cat. Make a frightening, fake jaguar skin.

**Warriors tried to capture enemies alive so that priests could kill them later, as sacrifices.**

**You will need:**
- White cotton fabric
- Sewing scissors
- Pencil
- Black marker
- Acrylic or poster paints
- Paintbrushes
- Two pieces of red ribbon

**❷** In pencil, draw on the body, tail, front legs and head. Draw dots all over your jaguar's body.

**❶** Fold the fabric diagonally to make a large triangle. Now cut along the fold.

**3** With a black marker, carefully go over all your pencil lines so the jaguar's features really stand out.

**4** Mix up orange paint and colour in the jaguar. Don't go over the black lines! Add the spots with black marker.

### Did you know?
Jaguar knights were sent on secret missions after dark and used to whistle to communicate.

Put on your jaguar cloak and feel strong and brave, just like an Aztec warrior.

**5** With scissors, cut a tiny hole on each side of the jaguar's head. Thread red ribbon through each of the holes.

# Japanese banner

In Japan, on Children's Day, children hang up fish-shaped flags on poles outside their homes to bring them good luck. Here's how to make your own fish banner that you can hang up in your room or classroom.

### What you need:
- Coloured tissue paper
- Glue
- Scissors
- Thin cardboard

**Japanese fish banners**

1. Cut three shapes out of tissue paper, copying the shapes in the picture below. Choose a different colour for each. The fish will fold along the centre, so make sure the pieces are big enough.

### Top tip
When cutting out the scales, fold the paper over so that you can cut lots of scales at once.

160

**2** Glue the tail onto one end of the long section, and the head onto the other end.

**3** Use your scissors to cut out lots of semicircles of tissue paper for the scales of the fish.

**4** Cut out four large circles and two smaller circles to make the eyes. Glue them to the head of the fish.

**5** When you have enough scales, add them to the long section of the fish. Glue them from the tail upwards, and slightly overlap each row onto the previous one – just like real fish scales.

**6** Fold the fish along the centre and glue the bottom edges together. Glue a ring of cardboard inside the mouth.

# Indonesian puppets

One of the world's oldest traditions of storytelling, shadow puppets have been popular entertainment in Indonesia for more than 1,000 years. They are called Wayang Kulit. Here's how to make your own Indonesian-style shadow puppet.

**You will need:**
- Coloured construction paper
- Paper
- Cardboard
- Pencil
- Scissors and craft knife
- Paper fasteners
- Wooden dowel or wooden skewers
- Adhesive tape
- White sheet
- Electric light

1 Sketch your puppet design roughly on paper. Give it a long nose, long, curling hair and a curving body and legs.

**An Indonesian shadow puppet show**

**2** When you are happy with your design, draw the figure on cardboard. Draw the arms separately and divide each arm into two parts – shoulder to elbow, and elbow to hand. Round the ends and cut out all the pieces. Ask an adult for help with the craft knife.

**3** Tape a stick down the back of one of the puppet's legs, so that the audience cannot see the stick.

**4** Join the arms to the body at the shoulder with paper fasteners. Join the lower and upper parts of the arms at the elbow.

**5** Tape a thin stick to each of the puppet's hands so you can move its arms.

**6** To put on a show, suspend a thin white cotton sheet between two chairs. Make sure there are no wrinkles in the sheet. Shine an electric lamp onto the back of the sheet. Kneel down and work the puppet above your head so that your audience see the puppet's shadow. Use one hand to operate one arm, and the other hand to operate the other arm and the head.

# Wear a Jarl's helmet

Jarls wore strong metal helmets to protect their heads and scare their enemies. No one will recognize you behind this nose guard!

You will need:
- Balloon
- Newspaper
- PVA mixture
  (3 parts pva, 1 part water)
- Scissors
- White cardstock
- Pencil
- Craft knife
- Glue
- Paint and paintbrushes

This helmet was designed to give extra protection to the wearer's eyes and nose. The crest on top helped guard his brain.

This detail from the Bayeux Tapestry shows Norman warriors sailing their warships to invade England.

**1** Blow up a balloon. Dip strips of newspaper into PVA mixture. Stick them to the top half of the balloon.

**2** Build up several layers of papier-mâché strips. Leave to dry. (This may take several hours.)

### Did you know?
Viking raiders captured people and then demanded a ransom (blood money) to free them alive.

**3** Pop the balloon and remove it. Use scissors to trim the jagged edges all the way round.

**4** Draw the eye and nose piece onto cardstock. Ask an adult to cut it out with a craft knife.

**If you want your helmet to shine, ask an adult to spray paint it for you. Make sure they do it outside!**

**5** Glue the eye and nosepiece to the papier-mâché helmet. When the glue is dry, paint the helmet gold.

# Stained glass

Stained-glass windows decorated churches and cathedrals in **medieval** times, and still do today. Make your own window and watch it glow when the light streams through it.

### You will need:
- Black construction paper
- White pencil
- Craft knife
- Scissors
- Coloured tissue paper or coloured cellophane
- Glue
- Fine black felt-tip pen

**1** Plan your picture first. Keep it simple, with bold lines and leave a 1–2-inch (2½–5 centimetre) border around it for the frame. Now, lightly draw your design on black construction paper with a white pencil. Leave a gap of ¼–½ inch (6–12 millimetre) between the different colours.

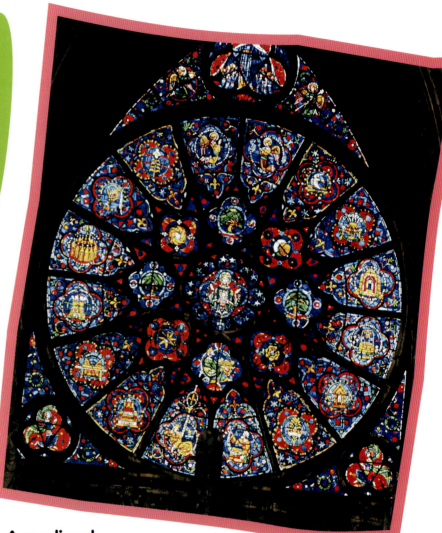

**A medieval stained glass window**

### Take care!
You will need an adult to help you with this project.

**2** Once you are happy with your design, go over the lines again, this time marking them with bold, white outlines.

**3** Ask an adult to help you cut out your design with a craft knife. Use a cutting board or several layers of newspaper.

**4** Cut tissue paper or cellophane to fit over each window in the paper. Put the pieces in place without glue first to check that they will fit over the holes.

**5** Glue each piece onto the back of the paper. Put glue around each hole, and try to keep glue off the front of the window.

**6** Hold the window up to the light. The light will shine through the cellophane, making the colours glow.

### Top tip
As you cut out more construction paper, the frame becomes fragile. Keep a heavy book over the frame so it does not rip while you cut out the remaining pieces.

167

# Moroccan tile

In countries such as Morocco, geometric patterns are used to create beautiful tiles.

**Take care!** You will need an adult to help you with this project.

### You will need:
- Thick cardboard, 5 ½ inches (14 centimetres) square
- Craft knife
- Masking tape
- Sponge or roller
- Ceramic paint (oil-based or water-based)
- Turpentine (for oil-based ceramic paints. Handle with care!)
- Plain white tile, 6 inches (23 centimetres) square
- Felt

A Moroccan tile

**1** Plan out a tile design and practise drawing it. When you are happy with it, draw it onto your cardboard square.

### Top tip
If you use oil-based paint, ask an adult to clean your brushes in turpentine. A cotton bud dipped in turpentine will wipe away mistakes.

**2** Ask an adult to help you cut around the lines with a craft knife. Use a cutting board.

**3** Tape the edges of the stencil you have made to a plain, white-ceramic tile.

**4** Dab ceramic paint onto the tile through the stencil with a small sponge, brush or roller. Try to fill all the gaps with paint.

**5** Remove the stencil. Let the paint dry if it is oil-based, or ask an adult to help you to fire it in the oven if it is water-based (following the instructions on the pack).

**6** Cut out a square of felt. Glue it to the back of your tile so you can put it on a table without scratching it.

# Make your own papyrus paper

The Egyptians invented paper. They made it from strips of papyrus reed soaked in water, then pressed together. Try making your own!

**To make papyrus (the first paper) the Egyptians cut thin strips of papyrus reed stalk, soaked them, laid them flat, then pressed them together.**

**An Egyptian farmer using a plow pulled by oxen to prepare his fields for planting crops. His wife walks behind him, scattering seeds on the freshly plowed earth.**

## You will need:
- Sheet of pale green paper
- Sheet of dark green paper
- Scissors
- PVA mixture (3 parts PVA, 1 part water)
- Plastic tray
- Paper towels

**1** Draw a ½ inch (1 centimetre) margin along the long edge of one sheet and along the short edge of the other.

**2** Cut ½-inch (1 centimetre) strips across the sheet to the long margin. Cut strips up the other sheet, to the margin.

**3** Weave the two pieces of paper together. Weave each strip over, then under, along the row.

**4** Fill the plastic tray halfway with the PVA mixture. Place your paper completely in the PVA mixture.

### Did you know?
Egyptian farmers kept cats to protect their grain stores from rats and mice. The Egyptian word for cat was 'miw'!

**Impress your friends with your handmade notepaper.**

**5** Pat your paper with paper towels to remove excess moisture. Hang to dry over a sink or tub.

171

# Russian egg

The first Fabergé egg was made in 1885, when the Russian Tsar, Alexander III, commissioned a jewelled Easter egg for his wife from the goldsmith Carl Fabergé. Here's how to 'blow' a real egg and decorate it in the style of a fabulous Fabergé egg.

You will need:
- Raw egg
- Pin
- Bowl
- Enamel paints
- Dried lentils, peas or beans
- Stick-on gems

1 Use a pin to push small holes through the top and bottom of the egg.

**The original Fabergé eggs were made in enamel and decorated with metals, such as silver, gold and copper, and precious stones.**

**2** Hold the egg over a bowl and gently blow through one of the holes. The contents of the egg will dribble out until the egg is empty.

**3** Holding the egg gently, paint the shell.

**4** Decorate the egg using lentils, seeds, sequins or stick-on gems for jewels. Carefully dot on glue and press one gem, seed or sequin in place at a time.

### Top tip
Use tweezers to pick up tiny seeds or gems, dip them in glue (or paint a layer of white glue on the egg first with a brush), and then drop them into place.

# Gladiator shield

A gladiator's shield was his best friend – it was the only thing between him and certain death!

This Secutor (Pursuer) gladiator wears a heavy helmet and metal leg guards. He is armed with a sharp sword and protected by a huge, curved shield.

### You will need:
- Big sheet of cardboard
- Ruler
- Scissors
- Marker
- Paint and paintbrushes
- Compass
- Double-sided tape
- White cardstock

**1** Cut a 24 x 16-inch (60 x 40 centimetres) rectangle from cardboard. Inside the rectangle, draw a big oval that touches the edges.

**2** Cut out the oval, then paint it yellow and let it dry. Now, paint on a red cross as shown.

There were five different kinds of gladiators. This Retarius (Net-man) has no helmet or body armor. His only weapons are a spear and a net.

### Did you know?
Roman actors invented new plays, called pantomimes, based on comic, acrobatic dance.

**4** Draw a 4-inch (10 centimetre)-diameter circle on cardstock. Cut it out, paint it brown, and when it's dry, stick it to the centre of the shield.

**3** Paint two diagonal lines that cross in the middle. Now paint a red border around the rim.

**5** Cut out a rectangle of cardstock. Use it to make an arm handle on the back, as shown.

Feel as brave as a gladiator as you carry your shield.

175

# Materials kit

In this section you will find out to make collages, build three-dimentional models, and create unusual effects using a variety of materials from straws to sequins! Here are some of the things you will need to get started.

**Top tip**
Don't forget to spread out some newspaper to work on, and wear an apron to keep your clothes clean.

**Paper and cardboard**
For many of the projects you will need:
- Thin cardboard or thick white paper
- Coloured paper
- Tissue paper
- Construction paper
- Thick cardboard from old boxes

But you can use all kinds of paper in your artwork such as newspaper/magazines, shiny card, tracing paper, crepe paper, brown paper, wallpaper, sandpaper, lacy doilies, used stamps, sweet wrapper, kitchen towel or blotting paper, tin foil, bubble wrap, cereal packets, egg boxes and kitchen roll tubes, etc.

**Safety scissors**

## Other basics
- Safety scissors
- Sticky tape
- Felt-tip pens
- Pencils and ruler
- Wax crayons
- Poster/acrylic paints and brushes
- White glue

You will also need some extra items, which are listed separately for each project.

## Frame it!
Choose your best work to frame in a simple or decorated card border. Start your own gallery!

## Bits and bobs
Keep a box of things with an interesting texture or shape. For example:
- Sequins, buttons and beads, shells, dried beans and seeds
- String, wool, ribbon and embroidery thread
- Nails, screws and paperclips

## Tools and brushes
Ordinary brushes are useful for backgrounds and details, but you might also want some unusual tools. Straws are good for blowing paint and for making paper quills. Toothpicks are good for scraperboard pictures.

**Sequins**  **Glue**

**Loom weaving**

**Masking and sticky tape**

## Take care!
Some projects involve cutting, gluing or spraying. Always ask an adult for help when you see this sign.

# 'Me' collage

Tell a story about yourself through a collage. The **theme** could be a birthday, a favourite hobby, a holiday – or what about your favourite things? Here are some things you will need:

### You will need:
- Materials for your collage
- Cardboard or posterboard

### Top tip
Always ask an adult for help with cutting and gluing.

### Football collage ideas
A football collage could include:
- Team photos
- Scraps from a football programme
- Ticket stubs from a match
- Newspaper headlines about football stars
- Fabric from an old football shirt
- Shoelaces

**1** Collect lots of things that tell a story. If you're not sure what to do, look at the pink and orange boxes on these pages for ideas.

**2** Arrange all the things you have collected on a cardboard **mount board**. Move them around until you are happy with the way they look.

**3** Glue down all the things to your piece of mount board with white glue. Glue a small area at a time.

### Click for Art!
To see a photocollage by David Hockney, go to http://artlex.com/ and search for 'Photocollage'.

Fun collage made from ticket stubs, postcards, and other holiday souvenirs

## Holiday collage ideas
- Photographs from travel brochures or magazines
- Ticket stubs and luggage tags
- A sprinkling of sand and shells
- Food and sweet wrappers
- Postcards and stamps
- Foreign coins

179

# Magazine collage

Make a collage from scraps cut or torn from magazines. Choose a theme you find interesting – this one is about food. Look at the collage themes box for other ideas.

### Collage themes
- Animals
- Ballet
- Cars
- Colours
- Dinosaurs
- Dogs
- Faces
- Flowers
- Sports
- Happiness
- Horse-riding
- Robots
- Space
- Winter

### You will need:
- Plenty of old newspapers and magazines
- Cardboard or posterboard

**1** Find pictures in magazines about your theme. Using safety scissors, cut out as many pictures as you can.

**2** Arrange the pictures on your mount board until you like the way they look.

**3** Glue the pictures onto the mount board.

**Click for Art!** To see collages by Picasso, go to **www.tate.org.uk**, click on 'Tate Collection' and find Picasso on the Artists 'A-Z'.

# 3-D pictures

To make a picture stand out from the cardboard mount:

**1** Glue the picture onto lightweight cardboard. Cut out around the picture.

**2** Fold a strip of cardboard in half, then in half again. Open it out a little, so it looks like a chair with the bottom folded under.

**3** Glue the flat part at the top to the mount board.

**4** Glue the picture to the raised part that sticks out at the front.

**Food collage using pictures cut from magazines**

# Paper collage

You can use all kinds of paper in a collage. Collect plain coloured paper, construction paper, wrapping paper, wallpaper, sweet wrappers, tissue paper and newspaper.

## Paper parrot

**1** First plan your picture. Draw the picture lightly with a pencil on the mount board.

### You will need:
- Different colours and textures of paper for the collage
- Cardboard or posterboard

### Top tip
Try using layers of coloured tissue papers so the top colour mixes with the colour below.

This parrot has been made from different kinds of paper, cut into shapes and then glued in place.

**Click for Art!** To see a collage by Matisse, go to www.tate.org.uk click on 'Collection', then search 'Matisse/The Snail'.

**2** Using safety scissors, cut out the different kinds of paper into the shapes you want for each part of the picture.

**3** Move the pieces of paper around on your drawing until they look right.

**4** Glue down the paper shapes, one at a time. To overlap shapes, glue larger pieces first, then smaller ones on top.

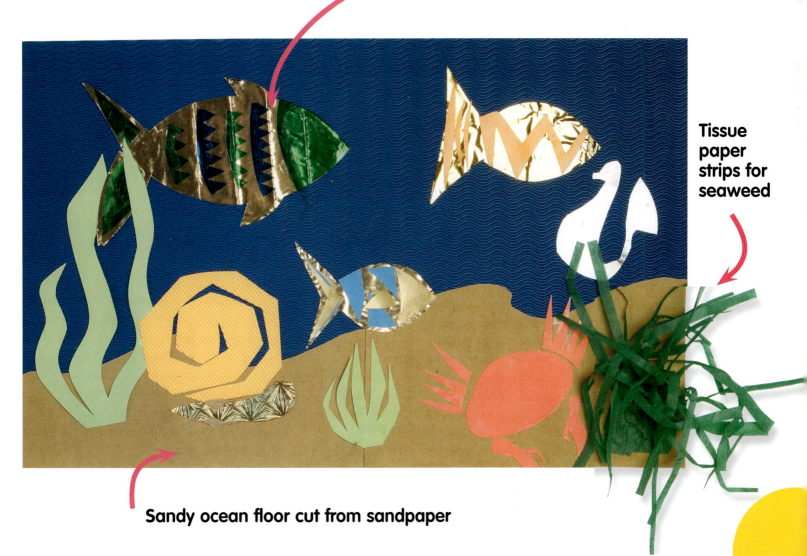

**Fish shapes cut from foil**

**Tissue paper strips for seaweed**

**Sandy ocean floor cut from sandpaper**

183

# Collage face

The collage face on page 185 was made from cardboard that was cut, folded and rolled in different ways.

**Cardboard crazy!**
How many types of cardboard can you find? Try collecting:
- Empty food boxes
- Cardstock
- Corrugated cardboard
- Toilet-paper rolls
- Shaped cardboard used for packing
- Lightweight white or coloured cardboard

There are lots of ways to make cardboard into different shapes.

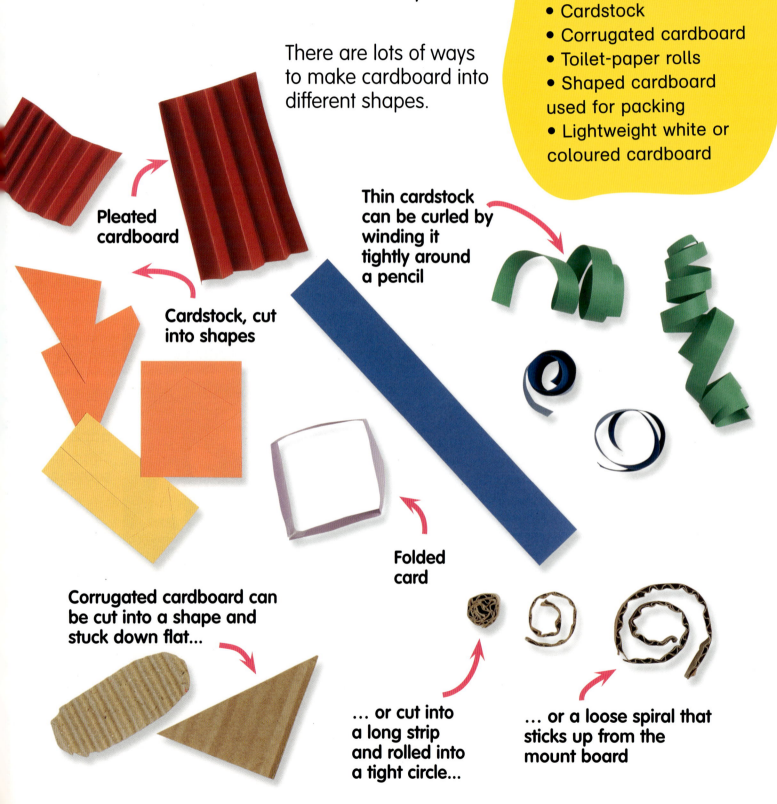

**Pleated cardboard**

**Cardstock, cut into shapes**

**Thin cardstock can be curled by winding it tightly around a pencil**

**Folded card**

**Corrugated cardboard can be cut into a shape and stuck down flat...**

**... or cut into a long strip and rolled into a tight circle...**

**... or a loose spiral that sticks up from the mount board**

184

# Food collage

It's fun to mix different materials and objects in a collage. Here's how to make a picture from scrap materials you may find around your home.

**You will need:**
- Dried food (see box)
- Black paper
- Cardboard for the mount
- White or yellow pencil
- Tweezers

**1** Glue the black paper onto a strong piece of cardboard as a mount board.

**2** Plan your picture on a piece of white paper first. When you are happy with it, draw it onto the black paper with a white or yellow pencil.

**3** Choose dried foods for the different parts of your picture. Sprinkle a few beans, lentils or seeds in each area to remind you what goes where.

### Food collage ideas

Food collages work best if you choose a simple pattern or picture. For example:

★ a flower
★ a tiger
★ a lizard
★ a snake with a zigzag pattern on its back

### Top tip

To avoid sticky fingers and messy patches of glue, use tweezers to position items on your collage.

186

Food collage with border made from pasta wheels

**5** Leave the collage flat until the glue has dried completely.

**4** Spread glue thickly over a small part of the picture. Sprinkle small seeds over the glue.

### Dried foods
- Red and green lentils
- Dried beans and peas
- Pasta shapes and spaghetti
- Black, white and brown rice
- Sunflower and poppy seeds
- Pine nuts

# Fabric collage

Collages made out of different fabrics are great to look at – and to touch!

## Collecting fabrics

Look out for fabrics with different textures, such as scratchy hessian, smooth silk and soft furs. Buy leftover pieces from shops or junk sales, or cut up old clothes – but always check with an adult first!

### You will need:
- Scraps of fabric
- Wide-eye needle and thread (optional)
- Thick cloth or cardboard for the mount

## Working with fabrics

You can use fabrics in a similar way to paper:

- **Pleating:** Glue the fabric down as you pleat it, or tack it with big rough stitches using a needle and thread.

- **Scrunching:** Crumple the fabric and glue it down.

- **Twisting:** Twist the fabric, then glue it in place.

- **Plaiting:** Plait strands of different fabrics into one.

- **Cutting:** Cut fabric into shapes to stick onto another material, or cut holes so you can see through to the fabric below.

**1** Plan your picture and draw it lightly onto the mount.

**Click for Art!**

To see fabrics used in a collage, go to www.wetcanvas.com/Articles2/4220/289/page5.php

**2** Using safety scissors, cut the fabric into shapes.

**3** Arrange the shapes on the mount until you are happy with the way they look. See the pink box for ways of giving your collage an interesting 3-D effect.

**4** Glue down the shapes, one small area at a time.

**Top tip**
If you don't want edges of cloth to fray, cut your fabric with pinking shears to give a zigzag edge.

**Flowers made from scrunched-up scraps of brightly coloured fabric**

**Clouds made from scraps of netting and lace**

**Sheep's soft coats made from wool**

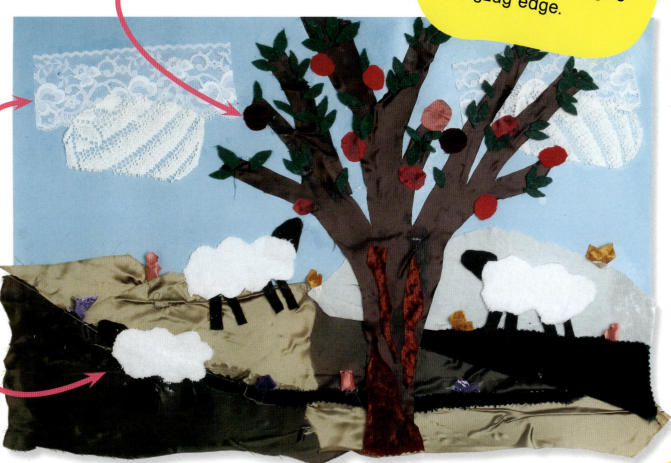

# Nature sculpture

Have fun making outdoor sculptures from smooth stones, fallen flowers and leaves, twigs, moss or feathers. You can find all the things you need for free in parks, woods, fields or your own garden!

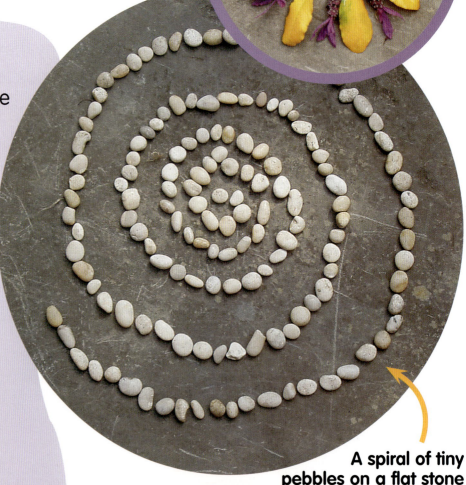

A spiral of tiny pebbles on a flat stone

### Sculpture tips

Natural materials can make great outdoor sculptures. Here are some ideas to start you off:
- Arrange berries in a pattern on moss.
- Overlap fallen leaves in the shape of a circle or a star.
- Arrange flower petals on a stone or rock.
- Make rows of pebbles or shells on the beach.
- If it's been snowing, make a sculpture out of snow.

If it's been raining, trace lines in mud with a sharp stone or twig, then add a pattern of fallen leaves.

### Changing nature

Ask a grown-up to photograph your nature sculpture. Go back to it the next day and take another photograph to show how it has been changed by wind, rain or animals.

**Click for Art!**

To see nature sculptures by Andy Goldsworthy, go to www.sculpture.org.uk/image/000000100091

**Colourful petals and leaves on grass**

**Shells arranged in the shape of a star**

191

# Thumb pot

This project shows you how to make a simple clay pot and decorate it with lively colours and patterns.

**You will need:**
- Air-drying clay
- Modelling tools

**1** Roll the clay into a ball between the palms of your hands. It should be about half the size of a tennis ball.

**2** Holding the ball in one hand, push the thumb of your other hand into the middle of the clay.

**3** Open out the middle of the pot by gently pinching the sides between your thumb and fingers. Keep turning the pot as you pinch, to keep the sides the same thickness.

**4** When you like the pot's shape, flatten the bottom by tapping it gently on a flat surface. Let it dry out a little, then decorate it using modelling tools, or by adding pieces of clay.

**Add simple shapes like this star to decorate your pot.**

**Click for Art!** To see examples of clay pottery, go to www.thebritishmuseum.ac.uk/compass/ and search for 'clay pot'.

## Top tip
At step two, don't press down too hard with your thumb or you'll make a hole in the bottom of your pot!

# Decorating your pot

When your clay pot is almost dry, decorate it with a **relief** pattern or press patterns into the side with modelling tools. If you don't have special pottery tools, use:
- the tip of a pen or pencil
- a large nail
- the end of a ruler
- a blunt metal knife or fork

**5** When the clay is completely hard, paint your pot with poster paint and let it dry. Finish it off with a coat of craft glue mixed with a little water.

'Studs' made from flattened balls of clay

Long thin snakes of clay stuck on with a little water

# Aztec monkey pot

Make a clay pot using the same coil technique as the Aztecs. Ozomatli (Oh-zoh-maht-lee), the Monkey god, protected art, games and fun.

### Did you know?
Traveling merchants walked barefoot as far as 30 miles (48 kilometres) a day to bring goods to sell at markets.

**Buyers and sellers hoped to get a good deal at the market.**

**Aztec traders brought this monkey pot from the city of Texcoco to sell. It is carved from shiny black obsidian (stone produced by erupting volcanoes).**

### You will need:
- Air-drying clay
- Modelling tools
- Black acrylic paint
- Paintbrushes

**1** Shape the clay into balls. Then use your hands to roll out the balls into several long thin 'sausages'.

**2** Fold in one end of the first sausage and then coil the rest around and around to build up the pot.

**3** If you need to add another sausage, just blend the end on. When the pot is big enough, smooth the sides.

**4** Roll a 5p-sized ball of clay for the head and four small sausages for the feet. Shape the head and feet.

**5** Attach the head and feet to the pot and smooth the joins. When the clay has dried, paint it black.

**To make your pot shine, use a clean brush to add a layer of PVA mixture (mix three parts PVA to one part water).**

195

# Roman plaque

Practise your Latin by making a Roman plaque for your bedroom door. Inscribe it with 'Salvete amici', which means 'Greetings, friends!'

You will need:
- Air-drying clay
- Rolling pin
- Ruler
- Plastic knife
- Modelling tool
- Pencil
- Paint and paintbrushes
- Length of string

Roman portrait of a woman writing poetry. She is using a pointed stick, called a stylus, to write on a wax-covered tablet.

Pupils and scribes jotted down notes on wax-covered tablets like this one.

① Roll out a ½ inch (1 centimetre) -thick slab of clay. Use a plastic knife to cut out a 6 x 3 inch (16 x 8 centimetre) rectangle.

**2** With a modelling tool, draw a ¾ inch (2 centimetre) border. In the centre of the plaque, inscribe your Latin message.

### Did you know?
Many languages still contain Latin words. Castle, memory, monster, mile, plumber, triumph, ultimate and extraordinary all come from Latin.

**3** Add pieces of clay to build up the border. With a sharp pencil, make a hole in each of the top corners.

**4** When your tablet is completely dry, paint it using Roman colours, such as black, red and white.

**Copy the Roman-style letters shown here to make your plaque as realistic as possible.**

SALVETE AMICI

**5** Once the paint is dry, thread the string through both holes, tie the ends together and hang up.

197

# Aztec rain god pendant

Aztec jewellery designs often featured gods. Make a pendant of Tlaloc, the god of rain and good harvests, in a few simple steps.

**You will need:**
- Air-drying clay
- Rolling pin
- Tracing paper
- Pencil
- Scissors
- Modelling tool
- Acrylic paints
- Paintbrushes
- String

The rain god Tlaloc (Tlah-lock) was known as 'He Who Makes Things Grow'. The Aztecs worshipped him because without rain, there would be no crops.

**Did you know?**
Human poo made excellent manure to help crops grow. Farmers collected the poo from public toilets in huts beside the canals!

**1** Warm the clay in your hands for a few moments and then roll out a slab about 1/3 inch (1 centimetre) thick.

**2** Trace the image of Tlaloc from the opposite page. Cut your tracing out and place on the clay.

**3** With a modelling tool, cut around your tracing. Cut zigzags along the top to make his crown.

**4** Use a pencil to make two eye holes right through the clay. Add his nose, mouth and teeth.

**5** When your pendant is dry, paint it bright colours. Once the paint is dry, thread string through the eyes.

**Knot the string and wear!**

199

# Thor's hammer

Viking blacksmiths poured molten metal into molds to make objects in special shapes. You can do the same with plaster of Paris!

**Viking men and women liked to carry amulets (lucky charms). Many were shaped like the magic hammer used by the god Thor when he fought giants and monsters.**

Little, metal statue of the goddess, Freya. Vikings said she made people, animals and plants grow strong and healthy.

### You will need:
- Non-drying clay
- Ruler
- Modelling tools
- Old pen top
- Plaster of Paris mixture (always follow the instructions on the packet)

### Did you know?
Some days of the week are still named after Viking gods, such as 'Thursday', which means 'Thor's day'.

**1** Shape non-drying clay into a small block. Press the sides against a ruler to make them smooth and straight.

**2** With a modelling tool, scoop out the hammer shape. Be careful not to go through the bottom!

**3** Press a pen top into the bottom of your mold to make circle patterns on your hammer.

**4** Following the instructions on the packet, mix up the plaster of Paris. Pour it up to the top of the mold.

**5** When the plaster of Paris has completely dried, carefully peel away the clay mold to reveal your amulet.

**You could use gold or silver paint to make your amulet look like metal.**

# Clay sculpture

People have been making clay models for thousands of years. For this project, you can use air-drying modelling clay, so you don't need to fire it in a **kiln**.

**You will need:**
- Air-drying clay
- Modelling tools

**1** Tear off a piece of clay and work it into the shape of a head with your fingers.

**2** Add features by sticking on extra pieces of clay or cutting away areas. Make hair by rolling the clay into strands.

**3** Stop when you're happy with how your model looks, and let the clay harden.

**Top tip**
Coat your finished model with glue mixed with a little water. The glue looks white at first, but dries to a clear, shiny finish.

**4** Paint your model with poster paints and let it dry.

**Click for Art!** To see sculptures by Henry Moore, go to **www.henry-moore-fdn.co.uk/** Click on the link to 'Perry Green', then on the interactive map, then on photos of sculptures.

## Animal shapes

Here are some simple animal shapes made out of clay:

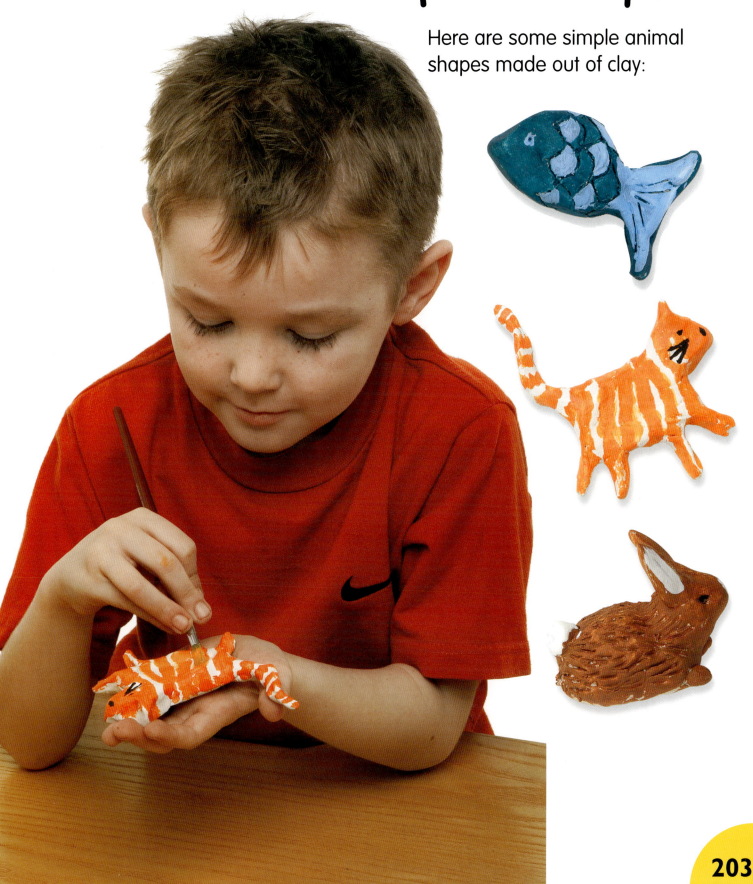

# Junk robot

You can make fantastic sculptures out of scrap materials! This robot has been made from cardboard boxes and tubes spray painted silver.

**You will need:**
- A large cardboard box
- Smaller boxes for the robot's lower body, hands and feet
- 9–10 toilet-paper tubes
- **Corrugated** cardboard
- Silver spray paint

**1** Glue down the open top of a cardboard box. Ask an adult to help you make a hole in the top and push in a toilet paper tube for the robot's neck. Secure it with sticky tape.

**2** Glue on a smaller cardboard box to make the lower part of the robot's body. Make two holes underneath and attach toilet paper tubes for the legs.

**3** Tape two toilet paper tubes together to make each of the robot's arms. Secure them to the sides of the robot's body with craft glue.

**Click for Art!** To see Picasso's 'Head of a Bull', a sculpture made with a bicycle seat and handlebars, go to **www.artviews.org/cosby.htm** and scroll down.

**Top tip**
For a shiny, metallic look, ask an adult to help you spray paint your robot silver.

**4** Cut out ears, eyes and a mouth from cardboard and glue them to a small cardboard box to make the robot's head.

**5** Ask an adult to help you cut a hole in the bottom of the head and attach it to the robot's neck.

**6** Glue on feet made from small cardboard boxes. Paint the robot when the glue is dry.

These robot eyes have been made from an empty egg box

Corrugated cardboard mouth

Feet made from shaped cardboard boxes

# Paper sculpture

This colourful bird has been made out of different kinds of paper that have been folded, creased or curled to look three-dimensional.

**You will need:**
- Coloured construction paper
- Scrunched-up newspaper
- Ribbon or yarn
- A stapler

## Bird of paradise

**1** Ask an adult to help you copy and enlarge the bird shape below onto two sheets of brightly coloured paper.

**2** Cut out one of the shapes and crease it with a ballpoint pen top, roughly following the dotted line. Do this several times until you can fold the paper so it bulges in the middle.

**3** Do the same with the other shape, but crease it on the opposite side.

**4** Ask an adult to help you staple the two pieces of paper together so the sides bulge out. Leave a gap at the bird's head and tail, then stuff it with scrunched-up pieces of newspaper.

**Paper beak folded and glued in a cone shape**

**Plastic 'googly eye' bought from a craft shop**

**5** Using safety scissors, cut out thin strips of coloured paper and wind them tightly around a pen or pencil so they curl.

**6** Glue long brightly coloured paper curls to make the bird's tail, and shorter curls for the wings.

**7** Hang the finished sculpture on the wall with a length of ribbon or yarn.

# Paper decorations

**1** Cut out six to ten strips of paper about 1-inch (2 ½ centimetres) wide.

**2** Leave two strips 12 inches (30 centimetres) long. Cut two strips 11 inches (28 centimetres) long, and cut two more strips 10 inches (26 centimetres) long.

**3** Arrange the strips with the long ones on the outside and the shorter ones in the middle.

**4** Staple the strips together at the top and bottom, so the shape balloons out, then hang it up.

207

# Cone hats

These cute hats are great to make – and fun to wear!

**1** Ask an adult to help you draw a big circle on a sheet of cardboard and cut it out with safety scissors. Cut a straight line from the edge of the circle to the exact centre.

**2** Overlap the edges to make a cone shape that fits your head, then secure the edges together with glue or tape.

**3** Paint your hat and decorate it with ribbons, sequins or glitter.

**4** Ask an adult to help you make a hole in each side of the hat. Cut a piece of elastic or ribbon and tie it through the holes.

### You will need:
- A large sheet of cardboard
- Ribbons, sequins, stick-on gems, glitter and feathers for decoration
- A length of elastic or ribbon

**Click for Art!** To see sculptural hats designed by Pip Hackett, go to www.vam.ac.uk/collections/fashion/ and search for 'Pip Hackett'.

# Wizard's hat

**Moons and stars cut from foil**

# Animal ears

**1** Using safety scissors, cut out a strip of cardboard 2 inches (5 centimetres) wide, and long enough to go around your head plus an extra 1 inch (2 ½ centimetres).

**2** Fit the strip around your head, and then ask an adult to staple the ends of the cardboard together.

**3** Cut out animal ear shapes from cardboard and glue them to the band.

**Rabbit ears painted with poster paints**

## Top tip

Try cutting out different sizes of circles. The bigger the circle, the wider or taller the hat. The wizard's hat was made from a circle measuring 39 inches (1 metre) wide.

# Pyramid

Make a gleaming, gold and white pyramid from cardstock. Once you've finished, you can hide your own treasures deep inside the pyramid.

**Three of the greatest Egyptian pyramids, at Giza. Originally, they were covered with slabs of white limestone and tipped with real gold.**

You will need:
- White cardstock
- Ruler
- Pencil
- Craft knife
- Scissors
- Double-sided tape
- Gold paint and paintbrush or gold paint pen

**1** Draw a triangle with 5-inch (12-centimetre) sides on cardstock. Ask an adult to cut it out with a craft knife and ruler.

**2** Place the triangle on a big sheet of card and trace it. Line it up beside the first outline and trace it again.

**3** Draw two more triangles using the same method. Now draw on a ¼ inch (5 millimetre) tab, as shown.

These tomb wall paintings show the kingdom of Osiris, the Egyptian god who helped the dead carry on living in the afterlife.

**4** Cut around the outer edge of your shape. Ask an adult to score along all the inner lines.

### Did you know?

The most famous rock tombs are in the Valley of the Kings, near Thebes. Tutankhamen was buried there in 1327 C.E., surrounded by wonderful treasures.

**5** Colour the tip of the pyramid gold using paint or gold pen. Add lines to show the limestone panels.

**Put a strip of double-sided tape along the tab. Then fold up the pyramid and stick the tab in place.**

# Ocean scene

First make and decorate this box for a **3-D** ocean scene – then turn the page to find out how to fill it with fish and other sea creatures!

**1** Cut off the flaps on the open side of the box, or fold them back and glue them to the sides.

### You will need:
- A large cardboard box
- Blue cellophane
- Newspaper
- Sandpaper, pebbles and shells

**2** Ask an adult to help you cut a rectangular hole in the top of the box to let in light at the back. Paint the box blue inside and out.

**3** Glue a piece of blue cellophane underneath the hole in the top of the box to create a watery blue light.

**4** Glue sandpaper, small pebbles and shells onto the bottom of your box to make a sandy seabed.

**Click for Art!** To discover the outdoor sculptures of Oldenburg and van Bruggen: www.metmuseum.org/explore/oldenburg/artist.html

**5** Scrunch up some old newspaper and pack it tightly into a corner of your box. Secure it in place with tape and glue.

**6** Tear more newspaper into strips and glue 2–3 layers over the scrunched-up newspaper, overlapping them as you go.

**7** When the glue is dry, paint the newspaper brown or grey, for rocks.

Now turn the page to find out how to make the sea creatures to put in the box.

213

# Ocean creatures

Now that you've made the box for your **3D** ocean scene, it's time to fill it with colourful fish and sea creatures.

**You will need:**
- Air-drying clay
- A plastic bottle
- Glitter glue
- A clear plastic food bag
- Tissue paper
- Transparent nylon line

## Clay crab and fishes

Use air-drying clay to make these sea creatures for your ocean scene.

Have fun decorating your models with bright colours and spotted patterns!

## Plastic bottle fish

These fish were cut out of a large plastic bottle, then painted with wavy and zigzag patterns.

Ask an adult to make a hole at the top of your fish, so you can hang it from the top of your box with transparent nylon line.

# plastic bag jellyfish

This sea snail was made from coloured air-drying clay

This seahorse was made from cardboard, built up with layers of glued newspaper strips and then painted

**1** Push some colourful scrunched-up tissue paper into a clear plastic food bag.

**2** Tie the bag around the middle, then cut the open end into strips for the jellyfish's tentacles.

**3** Glue on some big cardboard eyes or some 'googly eyes' from a craft shop.

**Click for Art!**

To design a 3D shape on an interactive art site, go to **www.nga.gov/kids/zone/zone.htm** and click on '3D Twirler'. You may have to download a program to work it.

# Special paint effects

You can give your paintings an extra twist by adding glitter or cornflour to paint, or sprinkling salt onto wet paint.

**You will need:**
- Glitter
- Cornflour
- Soft, wide brush
- Salt crystals

**1** Wet the paper all over with a soft, wide brush.

**2** While the paper is wet, drip blobs of paint in a circle and let them spread.

**3** Add a tiny dot of paint for the centre of each flower. Sprinkle grains of salt over the painted petals. Watch how the salt soaks up the paint and makes speckled marks on the paper.

## Flower painting

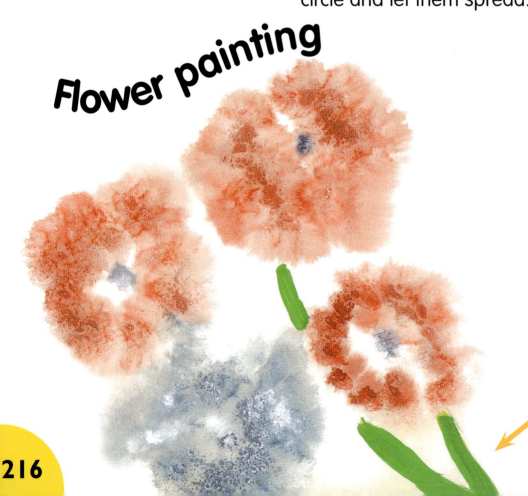

**When the paint is dry, add stems for the flowers with a thin brush**

**Click for Art!**

For a good art website that includes art galleries, art quizzes and information about artists and their work plus links to other art sites, visit www.scribbleskidsart.com

**Top tip**
Shake off the salt when the paint is dry, or leave it on if you want more texture in your painting.

## All that glitters

It's easy to make your own sparkly glitter paint. Just add glitter to acrylic or poster paint and paint it on with a brush as usual.

## Adding texture

To thicken poster paint, add a few spoonfuls of cornflour. Keep mixing until you have the texture you want. Paint with a brush as usual. If you like, make patterns in the paint with a stick or comb.

# Wax resist

Waxy crayons and watery paints don't mix – which means that if you draw a picture in crayon and then paint over the top, the drawing will show through.

You will need:
- A white wax crayon
- Paper
- Poster paints

**1** Use the wax crayon to draw the **outline** of the marrow and add some lines running along it.

**2** Paint yellow paint over the wax. The wax will **resist** the paint and the drawing will show through.

**3** Let the yellow paint dry. It will settle between the wax lines.

**4** When the yellow paint is dry, add some more wax lines.

**5** Add green paint. The wax allows the yellow to show through.

# Scraperboard

While watery paints slide off wax crayon, you can get quite different results if you cover the whole area with thick paint, and then scrape patterns on the surface.

### You will need:
- Heavyweight paper or posterboard
- Crayons or a candle
- Poster paint
- Brushes

**Make your own scraperboard**

1. Cover the paper with crayon, without any gaps. Whatever colour you use will show through – so choose bright colours or a white candle.

2. Now brush thick, black paint over the crayon surface, and let it dry. Repeat two or three times until the crayon is completely covered.

220

### Making pictures

**3** Scrape a pattern in the surface, using various tools – try the end of a paintbrush, a lollipop stick, or even a knitting needle.

## Top tip
Experiment with different scraperboard techniques. Instead of covering the crayon with black paint, use dark crayons and then cover them with white paint – black showing through white is very dramatic.

## Top tip
You could also try making lots of small scraperboard pictures rather than one large one. Try using lots of different colours of crayon – diagonal lines of red and orange make great flickering flame effects.

# Wax transfer

You can use wax crayons to make homemade transfers. Try out some simple designs, such as flower shapes, then when you have practised this technique, you can go on to make more detailed, colourful pictures.

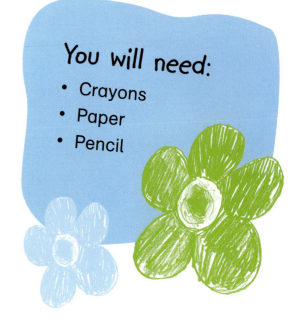

**You will need:**
- Crayons
- Paper
- Pencil

**1** Cover part of a piece of paper with crayon. Lay a clean piece of paper on top.

**2** Draw a simple design on top of the paper with the pencil. Fill it in, pressing hard.

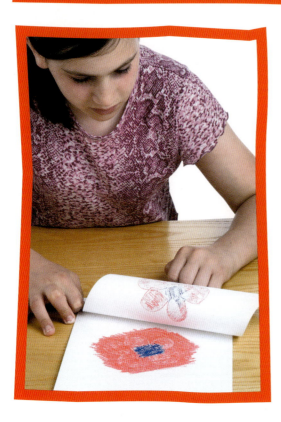

**3** Lift off the paper. The crayon should have transferred to the underside of the top piece of paper, leaving a pale copy on the piece below.

# Colour transfer

Using this wax transfer effect, you can turn a simple silhouette into an unusual colourful picture.

**You will need:**
- A sheet of parchment paper
- Heavyweight paper
- Crayons
- Pencil

**1** Lightly draw or trace a design on one side of the parchment paper. You don't need to keep the shapes simple.

**2** Turn the parchment paper over, and colour it with different colours of crayons. Try bands of colour, splodges, circles or squares.

**3** Place the parchment paper, crayon-side down, on a clean sheet of paper. Tape the edges so it doesn't slip. Now go over all the lines and areas of solid colour with the pencil, pressing firmly.

**4** Lift off the parchment paper to see the wax transfer beneath.

223

# Glitter project

Glitter comes in lots of different colours and can be used to make wonderful, sparkling pictures. Try this rocket idea.

**Paint and sparkle**

In this project, you use glue like paint to draw the shapes you want in your picture. Before the glue is dry, add some sparkle!

**What you need:**
- Coloured paper
- Pencil
- Glitter
- White glue
- Brush

Try making this rocket picture first. Then think of some other pictures that would look good in glitter.

**1** Draw the outline of the shapes in your picture in pencil. These are just guides for the glue stage.

**2** Use the brush to paint glue into your shapes. You could just use blobs or fill the shapes in.

**3** Before the glue dries, pick up some glitter and sprinkle it onto the picture. Use different-coloured glitters for different areas so the finished picture is bright. Leave the glitter on for a few minutes, before blowing off the extra glitter. The rest will have stuck to the glue and made a colourful image.

### Top tip
You can make your own glitter paint. Just mix some glitter with some glue and use a brush to put the sparkly paint on your paper. Now you can make your own glittering masterpieces.

# Material world

You can make fantastic pictures using fabric. Think about different looks and textures when choosing your materials. For example, cotton balls makes good fluffy clouds, or you could use lace for a more interesting effect. Have a go at creating your own country scene.

**You will need:**
- Cardboard
- Scissors
- White glue
- Pencil
- Fabric

**1** First, sketch the outlines of the scene on your paper in soft pencil. It is best to use cardboard because normal paper might tear.

**2** Cut out the large background pieces of fabric. You'll need blue for the sky, dark green for hills and light green for the fields.

**3** Now start adding all the details: a fence, a hedge, trees, animals in the fields, clouds and some flowers.

## Top tip
Collect old bits of fabric for your pictures. Scraps of white lace are excellent for making clouds or for snowy scenes. Ribbons are handy for creating flowers. Try experimenting with different fabrics for different objects.

## Top tip
When you have finished your fabric **collage**, you can paint it with clear **varnish**. This adds depth and makes the surface of the picture shine. The varnish effect looks great on a dark background.

# Paper sewing

Sewing isn't just for fabric. You can also use your needle and thread to make great designs on paper or cardboard. Always ask an adult for help when you want to use a needle. You could even use sewing in one of your paintings!

**You will need:**
- Posterboard
- Plain paper
- Needle
- **Embroidery** thread
- Adhesive tape
- White glue

### Embroidery house

This simple project will show you the basic method of paper sewing. Try some other designs.

**1** Draw a simple design on paper. Tape it over the posterboard, and sew thread through the paper and into the board. Discard the paper.

**2** On the back of the posterboard, neaten the loose threads. Knot the ends, cut the excess, and put small pieces of tape over the joins.

**3** Finally, cut another piece of posterboard slightly larger than the one with the sewing on it. Glue the sewing picture onto this.

## Stitching decorations

There a lots of variations you can use with paper sewing. Try putting colourful beads onto the thread and making zigzag patterns. You can use thread to make decorative borders to your cards and letters – just make sure you use thick enough paper to hold the thread.

## Paper pricking

You could also just use the needle to make holes in the paper that show up when light shines through them. This is a technique called paper pricking.

### Top tip
See if you can use sewing in some of your paintings or **collages**. You could use thread to make hair, colourful plants in the garden, or even a waterfall. Use different colours of thread together to get interesting results.

As well as decorative borders, you can use sewing to make colourful designs for birthday and Christmas cards. Using the same method as the project on page 228, you can make any shape or design you like.

# Collage

Paper and cardboard is cheap, colourful and easy to cut and paste, which makes it perfect for collage. Keep as many scraps as you can find – you never know when they may come in useful!

**You will need:**
- Coloured paper, magazines
- Posterboard or cardboard
- White glue

### Making a collage

**1** Sketch out a design on cardboard or posterboard.

**2** Cut or tear paper shapes to make up the design.

**3** Arrange the shapes until you are happy with the way they look and glue them in place.

## Mosaic

Try some different techniques in your collages. What about cutting out lots of small, coloured squares from old magazines and making them into an image like a Roman **mosaic**?

**Here is another colourful collage made with different types of paper.**

Experiment with other materials, too, such as buttons, kitchen foil and newspaper. You could also paint bits of paper different colours, tear them up, and then use them in your collages. Torn paper creates interesting textures.

**You can tear paper into the shapes of animals, flowers and trees.**

### Top tip

Once you have used paper to make colourful collages, you can go on to make paper sculptures. Cut out the shapes you'll need for your design, then colour them before you glue them together. You can make hair by cutting thin strips of paper.

**You could even make a sculpture out of paper.**

231

# Bits and pieces

Scraps and remnants from around the home look great in **collages**: fabric, lace, ribbons, **sequins**, pasta, beans, and toothpicks. You could probably make a collage from the contents of your wastepaper can!

**You will need:**
- Fluffy feathers
- String
- Toothpicks
- Coloured paper
- Dry leaves
- Beads
- Rice
- White glue
- Cardboard

### Perfect pets

**1** Draw the outlines of your picture with a pen then cut them out. Cut just inside the lines, so that the pen marks don't show – or turn your cut-out shapes the other way round.

**2** Arrange the main shapes on the cardboard. When you are happy with the way they look, glue them down.

**3** Now add a bead for the eye, rice flowers, toothpicks and string for the fence, coloured paper for the apples and feathers for the mane and tail.

# Still life

All the ingredients in this collage are easy to find. You can adapt it by mixing the collage with painting, and adding other natural materials, such as dried beans, seeds and pasta.

**1** Think how you could make what you've collected into a collage. Sketch the design on a piece of cardboard.

**2** Arrange your collection on the pencil outline. Glue it in place.

**3** You could leave your collage as it is. Or paint in a background and some flowers among your collage flower heads. Try adding colour to some of the objects in the collage if you like.

# Using photos

A camera can be useful in art. You can get all kinds of unusual effects if you combine photos with painting and collage. Keep your eyes open for interesting shots, and save photographs from magazines.

**Fantasy fun**

**1** Want a different home? Take a photo of your house and paint an unusual background to make it look as if you live somewhere different. Look in travel brochures for inspiration.

**2** Cut out the house and glue it to the background, or **superimpose** it using computer software. Send it as a postcard to family or friends.

**3** What about adding a friend or a pet to your picture? You could have fun playing with size and **proportions**, too! In your fantasy picture, objects can be as big or as small as you like.

# Picture strips

**1** Find two photos or magazine pictures, roughly the same size, and divide them into equal sections of ¾ inch (2 centimetres).

**2** Cut along the lines to make neat strips.

**3** Now glue the first strip from the first picture onto some card, followed by the first strip from the second picture. Keep going, using a strip at a time from each picture, until you've used all the strips.

You can use this effect to mix different animals, or alternate an animal with a photo of a celebrity or a landscape.

### Top tip
Try cutting the strips diagonally and horizontally, too.

235

# Glossary

**Aboriginal** the earliest people to live in Australia
**abstract** pictures that do not look like real objects
**accordian** folding a piece of paper or cardboard into small folds so that it has an accordian or fan-like shape
**acrylic** easy-to-mix paint that dries quickly and can be cleaned with soap and water
**Ancient Egyptians** the people who lived in Egypt a long ago and built the pyramids
**Ancient Greece** a civilization of more than 2,500 years ago, made up of hundreds of cities
**Athena** the Ancient Greek goddess of wisdom, represented by an owl
**Athens** the capital of Ancient Greece

**backdrop** the scenery in a theatre, at the back of the stage
**background** the area of a picture behind the main object
**batik** a way of decorating cloth using wax and coloured dye
**bison** a large, cow-like animal

**carnival** a happy festival, usually with a parade and music
**Celts** early tribal people of western Europe
**ceremonies** special formal events
**chalk** a soft stick of rock used for making soft, smudgy pictures
**charcoal** a drawing tool made from charred wood
**checked/checkered** having a pattern that is made up of squares
**collage** making pictures or patterns using different materials, such as paper and fabric, which are glued onto a background
**complementary colours** colours that work well together
**construction paper** a rough-textured paper – good for chalk and charcoal drawings
**corrugated cardboard** cardboard that has ridges in it
**cube** a square, six-sided, 3-D shape
**Cubism** a form of art in which pictures were made up from fragments of images

**Diwali** an important Sikh or Hindu festival, held during October or November
**dye** powder or liquid used to colour something, usually cloth

**embroidery** making pictures or patterns with sewing
**expressions** the look on a person's face when they are happy, sad, angry, etc.

**features** parts of the face, such as the eyes, nose and mouth, which make everyone look different
**felt** thick, fuzzy cloth
**fiend** an evil creature
**foreground** the area at the front of a picture
**frames** boxes that make up a page in a comic book
**fungicide** poison for killing mould

**geometric** a pattern made up of regular shapes

**highlights** the bright parts of a picture
**Hindu** relating to one of India's main religions, Hinduism
**horizontal** lines that run across the page from side to side
**hues** shades or tints of a particular colour

**Islamic** relating to one of the world's main religions, Islam

**kiln** a large, hot oven used to fire clay to make it last (air-drying clay doesn't need to be fired in a kiln)

**landscape** a scene – such as a country landscape, showing trees and hills, or an industrial landscape, showing factories and buildings
**latex paint** type of water-based paint, often used for painting walls
**legends** stories about the past

**Matisse (Henri)** French artist (1869–1954)
**Medieval** relating to the period of history known as the Middle Ages in Europe
**Metapec** name given to a traditional Mexican clay sun
**Morris (William)** British artist and writer (1834–1896)
**mosaic** picture or pattern made up of lots of small squares of colour
**mount board** piece of cardboard or paper onto which things are stuck
**mural** a decorative painting on a wall
**myths** stories about superhuman beings in the past

**Native American** the earliest people to live in North America
**nib** the writing end of a pen

**outline** the outer edge of an object – usually you draw this first and add the details later

**palette** specially made piece of wood or plastic for artists to mix their paint on
**pattern** repetition of shape, line or colour in a design
**personality** the way a person behaves
**Picasso (Pablo)** Spanish artist (1881–1973)
**portfolio** a case for storing and carrying your drawings
**primary colours** red, green and blue – the colours that are mixed to make all other colours
**proportion** the relative size of one thing to another

**relief** when part of a pattern or picture sticks out from the background
**resist** to not accept something – wax resists paint, which means it shows through the paint
**resist work** a form of printing in which you cover a raised surface with ink or paint and then press this down on a sheet of paper
**Romans** the people of Ancient Rome, whose capital was the city of Rome, around 2,000 years ago

**secondary colours** the colours that are made by mixing primary colours
**shade** to colour in part of your drawing to make that area darker
**shrines** sacred places
**silhouette** a solid picture that is done by drawing an outline and filling it in using one colour
**sketchbook** a book that is used for making quick sketches, which can be turned into proper paintings or drawings later
**sketch paper** very smooth paper – good for finished drawing, rather than rough work
**stencil** a shape cut out of cardboard which can be painted through or around
**Stone Age** early period of history, when humans used stone tools
**superimpose** to put one thing on top of another
**symmetrical** a shape that is the same on both sides

**tapestries** a heavy fabric picture or design made by weaving coloured threads
**texture** the surface of something – some papers have a smooth texture, other papers have a rougher texture
**theme** the subject of something, such as an idea for a film
**three-dimensional (3-D)** when an object has, or appears to have, height, width and depth

**varnish** clear paint that dries hard and protects the surface beneath it
**vertical** lines that run from top to bottom of a page
**Victorian** the period of history when Victoria was Queen of Great Britain

**Warhol (Andy)** American artist (1928–1987)
**watercolours** paints that mix with water, sold in tubes or blocks

# Index

Aboriginal art 132–133
abstract art 78–79
acrylic paints 58, 59, 60, 61, 177
African cloth picture 126–127
amulets 148–149, 200
animals,
　African art 126–127
　cartoons 38, 46–47, 50–51
　clay sculpture 203
　drawing 12–13
　headbands 209
　ocean scene 214–215
Australian art 91, 132–133
Aztec art 76–77, 98–99
　masks 146–147
　monkey pot 194–195
　pendant 198–199
　warrior costume 158–159

balloons 124
banners 160–161
bark rubbing 30
Bayeaux Tapestry 164
birds 14–15, 206–207
block printing 97, 108–109, 110–111
bodies 8–9, 10–11, 90–91, 185
bookplate 110
bracelet, Roman 136–137
brooch, Roman 130–131
brushes 58, 59, 60, 61, 124, 125, 177
buildings 16–17, 32–33, 50–51

camera 234
cardboard figure 10–11
cardboard printing 60, 61
cartoons 6–7, 38–39
carving, Viking 36
cave paintings 144–145
Cézanne 21
chalk 6, 7, 124, 125
chalk pastels 6
charcoal 6, 7
Chinese art 138–139, 156–157
cities 16–17, 32–33
clasp, Roman 130–131
clay mould 200–201
clay pendant, Aztec 198–199
clay plaque, Roman 196–197
clay pottery 142, 192–193, 195
clay sculpture 202–203
cloth picture 126–127
coil technique 194–195
collage 78, 178–179, 230–233, 234
　face 184–185
　fabric 188–189, 227
　food 180–181, 186–187
　magazine 180–181

　materials 176–177
　paper 182–183
　printing 122
　sewing 229
colour blending 66–67
combing technique 82–83
comic strip 54–55, 56–57
computers 234
craft foam 125
crayons 6, 7, 124, 177
crown, Roman 134–135
cubism 78
cutting board 124

Delaunay, Robert 17
designs 80–81, 108
Diwali 154–155
dot painting 66–67, 132–133
dragging technique 82–83
dragons 36–37, 138–139
dyeing material 140–141

eggs, Fabergé 172–173
Egyptian art 128–129, 148–149, 170
　pyramids 210, 211
enamel paint 124

Fabergé, Carl 172
fabric (see also material),
　collage 188–189, 232
　paints 61, 96
　printing 96
faces 24–25
　cartoons 42–43
　collage 184–185
　self-portrait 22–23
feathers 15, 76–77, 112, 232
felt 126, 127
felt-tip pens 6, 177
figures 26–27, 40–41
finger printing 90–91
fish 14–15, 160–161, 183
flags 160–161
flowers 20–21, 80–81, 112
food collage 180–181, 186–187
food printing 96–97, 114
fur 12–13

geometric patterns 154–155, 168
ghosts 50–51
gladiator's shield 174–175
glitter 216, 217, 224–225
glue 58, 59, 124, 177
Goldsworthy, Andy 191
gouache paints 59
Greek vase 150–151
grids 34–35, 88, 89
Groening, Matt 38

Hackett, Pip 208
hand printing 90–91

hats 208–209
headdress 76–77
helmets 164–165, 174
highlights 6
Hindu art 154–155
Hockney, David 178

Identikit set 24
Indian Rangoli 154–155
Indonesian puppets 162–163
inks 6, 59

jaguar costume 158–159
Japanese art 156–157, 160–161
junk 94–95, 204–205

landscapes 28
latex paint 125
laurel leaf crown 134–135
leaves 30
　drawing 18, 19
　nature sculpture 190–191
　patterns 80–81
　printing 60, 61, 92–93, 112, 113

marbling 104–105
masking tape 124, 177
masks 146–147
material (see also fabric),
　design 80
　dyeing 140–141
　pictures 226–227
　materials,
　collage 176–177
　drawing 6–7
　painting 58–59
　printing 60–61
　world art 124–125
Matisse, Henri 78, 182
metal work 200
Mexican art 142–143, 146
mirror printing 106–107
mirror writing 110
Moctezuma 76
modelling clay 124, 125
Monet 19
monkey pot 194–195
monoprints 118–119
monsters 50–51
Moore, Henry 203
Mori, Yoshitoshi 103
Moroccan art 168–169
Morris, William 81, 93
mosaics 152–153, 231
movement 10–11, 44–45
murals 88–89

nature printing 93, 112–113
nature sculpture 190–191
neck collar 128–129
Nefertari, Queen 128

238

Nero, Emperor 134
night-time scenes 17, 53
Norman warriors 164

objects 48–49
obsidian 194
ocean scene 212–215
oil pastels 6
Oldenburg sculptures 212

paint roller 124
paint spattering 62–63
painting,
　materials 58–59
　special effects 216–217
　using straws 64–65
paints 6, 58, 59, 124, 125
　printing 60, 61
　three-dimensional art 177
palettes 58, 59
paper collage 182–183
paper pricking 229
paper quills 177
paper sculpture 206–207, 208–209
paper sewing 228–229
paper stretching 84
papier-maché 124, 125, 150–151, 165
papyrus paper 170–171
pastels 6, 7
patterns 80–81
pencils 6, 58, 59, 124, 177
pendant, Aztec 198–199
people,
　cartoons 39, 50–51
　drawing 8–9
　poses 26–27
　self-portrait 22–23
photocollage 178
photographs 234
Picasso, Pablo 78, 180, 204
plaiting 188
plaque, Roman 196–197
plaster of Paris 200–201
pleating 188
Pollock, Jackson 63, 65
Pop Art printing 116–117
poster paints 6, 58, 59, 124, 125
　printing 60, 61
　three-dimensional art 177
potato printing 114–115
Potter, Beatrix 13
pottery 150–151, 192, 194–195
print collages 122–123
printing 60–61
　body parts 90–91
　foods 96–97
　junk 94–95
　leaves 92–93
　mirror 106–107
　monoprints 118–119
　nature 112

Pop Art 116–117
potatoes 114–115
stencils 102–103
string 100–101, 107
printing blocks 100, 101, 108–109, 110–111, 112
proportions 34
puppets 138, 162–163
pyramids 146, 210–211

Rangoli 154–155
Rauschenberg, Robert 65
relief patterns 193
reptiles 14–15
rock art 91
rock tombs 211
roller 60, 61
Roman art,
　gladiators 174, 175
　laurel leaf crown 134–135
　mosaics 152–153, 231
　plaque 196–197
　robe clasp 130–131
　serpent bracelet 136–137
Rothko, Mark 65
Russian art 172–173

salt 216, 217
scarab amulets 148
scenery, theatre 72, 73
scrap materials sculpture 204–205
scraper art 69, 83
scraperboard 220–221
scrunching 188
sculpture 190–191, 202–203, 204–205, 206–207
self-portrait 22–23
sequins 124, 177
Seurat 67
sewing paper 228–229
shadow puppets 162–163
shells 177, 191
shield 174–175
silhouettes 28, 31
*Simpsons, The* 38
sky painting 71
snakes 14, 98–99, 136–137
spatter art 62–63, 86–87, 121
speech bubbles 55
speed lines 11
sponge printing 60, 61, 111
spray paint 121, 165, 204
stained glass 166–167
stamps, sponge 111
stencils 63, 87, 102–103, 120–121, 169
still life 20–21, 233
stippling 120
Stone Age art 144–145
stone painting 74–75
storyboard 57
storylines 54–55, 56

storytelling 162–163
straw painting 64–65
string 100–101, 107, 124, 177
stylus 196

temples 146
tesserae 152
texture 6
　collage 231
　fur 12, 13
　painting effects 217
　paints 59
　three-dimensional art 177
theatre 72–73
thought bubbles 55
three-dimensional art,
　buildings 33
　materials 176–177
　ocean scene 212–215
　theatre 72–73
thumb pot 192–193
tiles, Moroccan 168–169
tissue paper 124
tombs, Egyptian 211
transfers 222
trees 18, 19, 30–31
Turner 71
Tutankhamen 211
twisting 188

vampires 50–51
van Bruggen sculptures 212
vase, Greek 150–151
viewfinder 28–29, 32
Viking art 36, 37, 165
　amulets 200–201
　dyeing material 140–141
　stones 74–75

wall paintings 211
wallpaper design 80, 81
wallpaper paste 124, 125
Warhol, Andy 116, 117
warrior costume 158–159
watercolours 6, 58, 59, 70–71, 84–85
Watteau 9
wax crayons 6, 177
wax resist technique 68–69, 218–219
wax tablets 196
wax transfer technique 222–223
Wayang Kulit puppets 162
weaving 177
Wedjat-eye charm 148
werewolves 50–51
witches 50–51
wizard's hat 209
world art 124
wrapping paper 103, 114, 121, 182
writing 156–157, 196

# Notes for parents and teachers

The projects in this book are suitable for use in the home or can be used as stand-alone lessons in the classroom. They can also be used as a part of other areas of study.

While the ideas in the book are offered as inspiration, children should always be encouraged to paint, draw, sculpt or create from their own imagination and first-hand observations.

## Sourcing ideas

All art projects should tap into children's interests, and be directly relevant to their lives and experiences. Try using stimulating starting points such as found objects, discussions about their family and pets, hobbies, TV programmes or favourite places.

Encourage children to source their own ideas and references, from books, magazines, the Internet or CD-ROM collections.

Digital cameras can be used both to create reference material (pictures of landscapes, people, or animals) and also used in tandem with children's finished work (see below).

Other lessons can often be an ideal springboard for an art project – for example, a geography field trip can be used as a source of ideas for a landscape picture.

Encourage children to keep a sketchbook to sketch ideas for future paintings and creations, and to collect other images and objects to help them develop their work.

Give children as many first-hand experiences as possible through visits and contact with creative people.

## Evaluating work

Arrange for the children to share their work with others, and to compare ideas and methods—this is often very motivating. Encourage them to talk about their work.

Show the children examples of other artists' paintings, sculptures, etc. – how did they tackle the same subject and problems?

Help children to judge the originality and value of their creations, to appreciate the different qualities in others' work and to value ways of working that are different from their own.

## Going further

Look at ways of developing the projects further – for example, adapting the work into collage, print making or ceramics.

Use image-enhancing computer software and digital scanners to enhance, build up and juxtapose images.

Show the children how to develop a class art gallery on the school website.